From Command To Collaboration:

A Journey In Modern Leadership

By

Mark Welsh

Dedication

This book is dedicated to the brave men and women who serve our country, both in uniform and out. To those who have walked the challenging path from military service to civilian life, your courage and adaptability inspire me every day.

To my father, whose quiet strength and unwavering support have been my compass through every storm. Dad, your example as both a veteran and a civilian showed me that true leadership is about integrity, empathy, and continuous growth. This book is a testament to the values you instilled in me.

To my family, whose love and patience have been the bedrock of my journey. Your sacrifices and understanding through the ups and downs of my career transitions have not gone unnoticed. This book is testament to you helping to overcome life's challenges.

And to all those who dare to lead, who strive to make a positive difference in the lives of others, whether in the military, in business, or in their communities. May this book serve as a bridge between worlds, helping us all to grow, adapt, and lead with both strength and compassion.

While this book draws heavily from my experiences transitioning from military to civilian leadership, its lessons are not confined to that specific journey. To every leader out there, regardless of your background or the path that brought you to leadership: this book is for you.

Whether you're a seasoned executive, a rising manager, an entrepreneur, or a community organizer, the principles of emotional intelligence, adaptive leadership, and collaborative problem-solving explored here are universally applicable. In our rapidly changing world, all leaders face the challenge of evolving their approach to meet new demands. This book is dedicated to every individual committed

From Command To Collaboration: A Journey In Modern Leadership

to that evolution, to becoming a more effective, empathetic, and inspiring leader in whatever context they serve.

Leadership is a journey, not a destination. This book is dedicated to all my fellow travelers on that journey. May we continue to learn, grow, and inspire each other along the way.

Acknowledgment

As I reflect on the journey that led to this book, I'm filled with profound gratitude for the many individuals who have shaped my path and supported me along the way.

First and foremost, I want to thank my father. Dad, your unwavering support, quiet strength, and the example you set as both a veteran and a civilian have been my guiding stars. You showed me that true leadership transcends any single context, and your belief in me has been a constant source of motivation.

To the military leaders who molded me during my time in the Army, particularly in the 82nd Airborne and during the Gulf War: your lessons in discipline, duty, and decisiveness under pressure have been invaluable. While this book explores how I adapted those lessons for civilian life, the core principles you instilled remain the foundation of my leadership philosophy.

I'm deeply indebted to the civilian leaders and mentors who patiently guided me through my transition from military to civilian. Your willingness to share your wisdom, challenge my assumptions, and support my growth was crucial in helping me navigate the complex world of civilian leadership.

To my colleagues and team members in various private and civilian organizations: your patience, feedback, and collaboration were instrumental in my evolution as a leader. You taught me the power of diverse perspectives and the importance of fostering a culture of trust and innovation.

To my close family - my wife, children, and sibling - your love, understanding, and unwavering support have been my anchor through every challenge and triumph. You've been there through moments of self-doubt, bursts of inspiration, crazy ideas, and adventures.

Finally, to you, the reader: thank you for joining me on this exploration of leadership. Whether you're a veteran transitioning to civilian life, a

From Command To Collaboration: A Journey In Modern Leadership

new manager finding your way, or an experienced leader looking to refine your approach, I hope this book serves as a helpful companion on your journey.

Leadership is a continual process of growth and learning. I'm grateful for every individual who has been part of my journey, and I look forward to the lessons yet to come.

With deep appreciation,

Mark Welsh

Table of Content

From Command To Collaboration: A Journey In Modern Leadership

From Command To Collaboration: A Journey In Modern Leadership

From Command To Collaboration: A Journey In Modern Leadership

Introduction:
From Military Command to Civilian Leadership

When I first stepped onto the soil of Fort Sill, Oklahoma, for Basic Training, I had no inkling of the profound journey that awaited me. The crisp uniform, the polished boots, the rigid posture—these were merely the outward symbols of a transformation that would redefine not only my career but my entire approach to leadership and life itself.

My name is Mark, and this book represents the culmination of decades of leadership experience forged through hard-earned lessons and marked by a dramatic transition from military command to civilian leadership. As you accompany me on this journey, you'll uncover how the principles I internalized in the military both aided and complicated my shift to civilian leadership and how I eventually crafted a more nuanced and effective approach to leading in the contemporary business landscape.

Like many, my military career began with the rigorous challenges of Basic Training and Advanced Individual Training. However, it quickly propelled me to the elite 82nd Airborne Division after the Jump School, where I learned that true leadership often requires being the first to leap from a plane at 800-1,200 feet. This early experience instilled in me the crucial lesson of leading by example—a principle that became the bedrock of my leadership philosophy throughout my career.

As I advanced through the ranks, I had the honor of attending a series of leadership courses that formed my understanding of what it actually means to lead:

- Primary Leadership Development School

- The Warrior Leader Course (WLC)

- Basic Non-Commissioned Officers Leadership Course

- Advanced Non-Commissioned Officers Leadership Course

- Basic Leader Course (BLC)

- Advanced Leader Course (ALC)

- Senior Leader Course (SLC)

- Many others

Each of these courses built upon the last, sharpening my leadership skills and expanding my worldview. They emphasized the critical importance of clear communication, adaptability, and making decisions under pressure—skills that would become essential in the years ahead.

My leadership journey took a profound turn during the Gulf War, where I served as a platoon leader. The "fog of war" isn't just a metaphor; it's a harsh reality that challenges every facet of a leader's abilities. In those intense moments, I grasped the true essence of responsibility and accountability. Every decision carried tangible consequences, and the gravity of those choices profoundly shaped my understanding of what it truly means to lead.

However, my military experience extended beyond combat leadership. I also attended the Recruiting and Retention School, where I learned vital lessons in motivation and persuasion. Serving as a helicopter crew chief and mechanic, I realized the critical importance of meticulous attention to detail and technical knowledge in leadership parts.

As my career progressed, I participated in the Organizational Leader Development Course, the Civilian Leader Career Broadening Program, and the Executive Leadership Development Program. These experiences began to link the gap between military and civilian leadership, offering insights that would prove invaluable as I transitioned later in my career.

From Command To Collaboration: A Journey In Modern Leadership

During my military career, I adopted key leadership principles that became the base of my approach:

1. Leading by example
2. Clear communication
3. Adaptability
4. Decision-making under pressure
5. Team building and cohesion
6. Responsibility and accountability
7. Mission focus
8. Risk management
9. Mentorship and development

These principles have served me well in the military, where the chain of command is unambiguous, and orders are executed without hesitation. However, as I would soon realize, the civilian world plays by a vastly different set of rules.

My transition to civilian leadership was anything but seamless. The strategies and tactics that had once propelled my success in the military often fell short in the corporate arena. I found myself grappling with the challenges of an environment where authority isn't absolute, where motivation extends beyond a mere sense of duty, and where the "mission" isn't always clearly defined.

This book chronicles that transition – the missteps I took, the lessons I absorbed, and the new strategies I crafted. It serves as a guide for anyone navigating the shift from a highly regimented leadership framework to one that demands greater adaptability, emotional intelligence, and cooperative problem-solving.

In the chapters that follow, we'll explore:

- The military mindset and its strengths and limitations in civilian contexts

- The early missteps I made in civilian leadership and what they taught me

- The power of asking rather than telling

- How to lead from within rather than from the front

- Techniques for fostering innovation and creative thinking

- The myth of multitasking and the importance of focused work

- The role of emotional intelligence in modern leadership

- How to build and lead high-performance teams in any setting

Whether you're a seasoned veteran transitioning to civilian life, a new manager finding your foothold, or an experienced leader aiming to refine your approach, this book delivers actionable insights and strategies for mastering leadership in today's world.

Leadership isn't a final destination—it's an ongoing journey of learning and adaptation. My path led me from the disciplined demands of military command to the nuanced challenges of civilian leadership, and I'm eager to share the valuable lessons I've gathered along the means.

So, gear up (in a metaphorical sense) and join me on this leadership journey. The road ahead might be tough, but the view from the top makes every step worthwhile.

Welcome to "From Command to Collaboration: Navigating the Journey of Modern Leadership."

Chapter 1:
The Military Mindset

Foundations of Military Leadership

The military has long been seen as a crucible for cultivating leadership, and this perception is well-earned. The principles of military leadership are grounded in centuries of tradition, honed through the harsh realities of combat, and continuously improved through intensive training and education.

When I first joined the Army, I was immediately struck by how pervasive military culture was. Every facet of our existence was dictated by a strict set of rules, expectations, and core values. I quickly realized that this structure wasn't merely about maintaining discipline; it was the very foundation upon which military leadership was built.

The core values of the U.S. Army—Loyalty, Duty, Respect, Selfless Service, Honor, Integrity, and Personal Courage (summarized by the acronym LDRSHIP)—were ingrained in us from the moment we arrived. These were far more than just words on a motivational poster; they were the principles that directed every action we took and every decision we made.

One of the first significant lessons in leadership I encountered came during a relentless field exercise in Basic Training. Our platoon had been trudging through thick underbrush for hours, with exhaustion setting in and tempers fraying. Then, abruptly, our drill sergeant ordered us to halt and gathered us together.

"Listen up," he commanded with authority. "Leadership isn't about being at ease. It's about doing what needs to be done, especially when the going gets tough." He then proceeded to meticulously demonstrate land navigation techniques despite being just as fatigued as the remainder of us.

This moment solidified a critical aspect of military leadership in my mind: the relentless dedication to the mission and to one's fellow soldiers, no matter the personal discomfort or obstacles one might face.

As I advanced in my career and participated in numerous leadership courses, I began to grasp that military leadership is anchored in several fundamental principles:

1. Chain of Command: The clear hierarchical structure that defines authority and responsibility.

2. Mission Command: The philosophy of empowering subordinate leaders to make decisions within the commander's intent.

3. Discipline: The bedrock of military effectiveness, ensuring that orders are followed and standards are maintained.

4. Training and Readiness: The constant preparation for the challenges of combat.

5. Esprit de Corps: The sense of pride, fellowship, and common loyalty shared by members of a particular group.

These core principles establish a unique leadership atmosphere, fostering decisiveness, sharp communication, and a deep sense of mission. Yet, as I would come to realize, they also build expectations and instill habits that can be difficult to adjust to in civilian life.

Key Principles of Military Leadership

Throughout my military journey, from my early days as a young soldier in the 82nd Airborne Division to leading a platoon during the Gulf War, I was consistently immersed in and required to demonstrate the fundamental principles of military leadership. These principles, which became deeply embedded through rigorous training and real-world experience, were the foundation of my leadership approach throughout my service.

From Command To Collaboration: A Journey In Modern Leadership

1. Lead from the Front: This principle was hammered home from the earliest days of my training. Whether it was being the first to jump from the plane during airborne operations or taking point on a patrol, military leaders are expected to lead by example, sharing in the risks and hardships of their troops.

2. Know Your People and Look Out for Their Welfare: In the military, unit cohesion is paramount. Leaders are expected to know their subordinates not just as soldiers but as individuals. This knowledge allows for better decision-making and fosters trust within the unit.

3. Keep Your Subordinates Informed: Clear communication is crucial in military operations. Leaders must ensure that their intent is understood and that relevant information flows both up and down the chain of command.

4. Ensure the Task is Understood, Supervised, and Accomplished: This principle emphasizes the importance of clear orders, proper oversight, and mission accomplishment. It's not enough to give an order; leaders must ensure its properly executed.

5. Train Your Subordinates as a Team: The military operates on the principle of collective effort. Leaders are responsible for developing their units into cohesive teams capable of functioning effectively under stress.

6. Make Sound and Timely Decisions: In combat situations, indecision can be fatal. Military leaders are trained to gather available information, make a decision, and commit to a course of action.

7. Develop a Sense of Responsibility in Your Subordinates: This principle is about empowering junior leaders and fostering initiative. It's closely tied to the concept of Mission Command.

8. Employ Your Unit in Accordance with Its Capabilities: Understanding the strengths and limitations of your unit is crucial for effective leadership and mission success.

9. Seek Responsibility and Take Responsibility for Your Actions: This principle encourages proactive leadership and accountability.

These principles transcended mere theoretical concepts; they became practical guidelines that I integrated into my daily routine. For example, during a particularly demanding training exercise as a young NCO, I consciously shared in every hardship my team encountered—from the scant field rations to the chilly, damp conditions. This visible commitment to "leading from the front" greatly enhanced morale and strengthened unit cohesion.

In a similar vein, the principle of "knowing your people" proved to be essential during my deployment in the Gulf War. By understanding the unique strengths and concerns of my platoon members, I could assign tasks more effectively and provide targeted support precisely where it was most required.

However, it is crucial to recognize that, while these principles served me well in a military setting, they would later require substantial adaptation in the civilian world—a challenge we will delve into in the following chapters.

Historical Context and Evolution

The principles of military leadership I learned and practiced did not arise in isolation. They are the culmination of centuries of martial tradition, honed and refined through numerous conflicts and evolving technologies.

The concept of military leadership has its roots in ancient civilizations. Sun Tzu's "The Art of War," composed in the 5th century BCE, continues to be a foundational text for military leaders today. Its focus on strategy, self-awareness, understanding the enemy, and adaptability remains applicable in contemporary contexts.

In the Western tradition, the Roman legions set a precedent for a disciplined, hierarchical military structure that would influence European armies for generations. The role of centurions—professional officers who led from the front—resonates in today's military leadership ideologies.

The evolution of military leadership gained momentum with the establishment of standing professional armies in the 17th and 18th centuries. Frederick the Great of Prussia, for example, underscored the importance of discipline and drill while also advocating for initiative among his officers—an early precursor to the Mission Command philosophy.

The American military tradition, which has significantly shaped my own experience, draws from these foundational elements but has its own distinctive evolution. The citizen-soldier ideal, embodied by George Washington's leadership during the Revolutionary War, highlighted the significance of character and civic virtue in military leaders.

The Civil War introduced substantial transformations in military leadership in America. The vast scale of the conflict and the influence of emerging technologies, such as the telegraph and railroads, necessitated a fresh approach to command and control. Leaders like Ulysses S. Grant illustrated the importance of strategic thinking and perseverance in this context.

The World Wars of the 20th century further revolutionized military leadership. The conception of Mission Command, or Auftragstaktik, developed by the German Army, highlighted giving subordinates a mission along with the freedom to achieve it as they saw fit. This principle would later be embraced and adapted by the U.S. military.

In my own experience, the post-Vietnam era marked a renewed focus on professionalism and education within military leadership. The formation of the All-Volunteer Force in 1973 necessitated a shift in leadership methodologies, emphasizing motivation and preservation.

The leadership principles I internalized were further influenced by my experiences during Operations Desert Shield and Desert Storm, where I served as a platoon leader. The complexities of coalition warfare and the demands of leading in a high-tech battleground environment required adaptability and effective communication.

More recently, the conflicts in Iraq and Afghanistan have once again reshaped military leadership, placing greater emphasis on cultural awareness, counterinsurgency strategies, and the complexities of unequal warfare.

Throughout this evolution, certain fundamental principles have remained unchanged—the importance of discipline, the necessity of clear command structures, and the value of leading by example. However, the application of these principles has continually adapted to address new technologies, shifting societal expectations, and evolving dangerous environments.

Understanding this historical context deepened my appreciation for the rich and resilient tradition of military leadership. It also equipped me, to some extent, with the ability to adapt these principles in the face of new challenges—a skill that would prove invaluable in my change to citizen leadership.

Case Studies in Military Leadership

Throughout my military career, I came across countless instances of both outstanding and subpar leadership. These real-life case studies acted as potent learning opportunities, demonstrating how leadership principles can be applied effectively in high-pressure scenarios.

Case Study 1: Operation Gothic Serpent

(Battle of Mogadishu, 1993)

While I wasn't directly involved in this operation, it was thoroughly analyzed in our leadership courses. The operation, which ultimately led to the events illustrated in Black Hawk Down, offered numerous critical leadership lessons:

1. Adaptability: When the original plan went awry, leaders on the ground had to quickly adapt to a rapidly changing and deteriorating situation.

2. Courage under fire: The actions of sergeants like Norm Hooten and John Belman in organizing the defense and rescue efforts exemplified the principle of leading from the front.

3. Mission focus: Despite overwhelming odds, the soldiers remained committed to their mission of rescuing their comrades, demonstrating extraordinary dedication and sacrifice.

The main lesson emphasized the critical role of training and unit cohesion. In tumultuous scenarios, soldiers depend heavily on their training, as well as their confidence in their leaders and comrades.

Case Study 2: Personal Experience in the Gulf War

During my placement as a platoon leader in the Gulf War, I encountered a situation that truly challenged my leadership abilities. Our mission was to secure a strategic crossroads, but the intelligence regarding enemy presence was ambiguous at best. I faced a critical decision: should I proceed with caution, potentially sacrificing the element of surprise, or act swiftly and risk falling into an ambush?

Drawing on the opinion of "Make Sound and Timely Decisions," I promptly sought input from my sergeants, evaluated the risks, and ultimately opted for a cautious advance, dispatching reconnaissance elements ahead of our main force. This choice proved advantageous when our recon team uncovered a small enemy unit preparing an ambush. Thanks to our careful approach, we managed to outflank them and secure the crossroads without suffering any casualties.

The key takeaway was the significance of making decisive actions based on the best available information and the importance of trusting and leveraging the expertise of my subordinates.

Case Study 3: Training Exercise Leadership Failure

Not every example of leadership shines positively; in fact, we often glean more insights from failures than from successes. During a comprehensive training exercise, I witnessed a company commander whose leadership approach was excessively authoritarian and rigid.

When confronted with an unexpected scenario introduced by the exercise controllers, this leader stubbornly adhered to the original plan, disregarding the valuable input from his platoon leaders, who possessed superior ground-level intelligence. This inflexibility led to the company decisively "losing" the exercise.

This unfavorable example underscored the risks of neglecting the opinion of "Employ Your Unit in Accordance with Its Capabilities" and emphasized the critical importance of being receptive to feedback from assistants.

These case studies, among countless others, reinforced the leadership principles we had studied in more formal environments. They illustrated that effective military leadership involves more than merely adhering to a set of rules; it requires the flexible and intelligent application of those principles in real-world contexts.

Strengths of the Military Approach

The military approach to leadership, shaped by the intense pressures of combat and refined over centuries of practice, boasts several unique strengths that make it particularly effective in its specialized operating environment.

Clarity of Purpose and Chain of Command

One of the most significant advantages of military leadership lies in the clarity it imparts. In the military, missions are unequivocal, the chain of command is clearly defined, and every member understands their role. This sense of clarity minimizes confusion and enables swift decision-making and action.

I witnessed this firsthand during an intricate multi-unit training exercise. Despite the chaos of simulated combat, each soldier understood precisely whom to report to and what their objectives entailed. This understanding enabled our unit to respond rapidly and effectively to evolving scenarios.

Emphasis on Discipline and Training

The military's unwavering commitment to discipline and training stands out as a crucial strength. This approach guarantees that soldiers can execute their duties proficiently, even in the most intense situations.

During my service in the 82nd Airborne, our demanding training regimen ensured that essential procedures—such as aircraft exit and parachute control—were so thoroughly ingrained that we could execute them accurately, even while jumping into darkness or under enemy fire.

Development of Mental Toughness and Resilience

Military leadership is highly effective at fostering mental toughness and resilience within both individuals and units. The demanding nature of military life and training cultivates a robust capacity to endure difficulty.

I witnessed this consistently during intense field exercises and deployments. Soldiers' ability to persevere through exhaustion, discomfort, and fear serves as a powerful testament to the success of military leadership in instilling mental toughness.

Emphasis on Teamwork and Unit Cohesion

The military's emphasis on teamwork and unit cohesion represents a vital strength. The connections forged among soldiers, particularly in combat units, cultivate a profound level of trust and mutual support, ultimately boosting overall effectiveness.

From my perspective, this sense of unit cohesion frequently became the crucial element that enabled us to thrive in difficult situations where individual efforts would have fallen short.

Clear Ethical Framework

The military offers a robust ethical framework for making decisions. Core values and an unwavering sense of duty steer actions and choices, even amid morally intricate situations.

Throughout ethical decision-making exercises in leadership training, this framework has been essential for maneuvering through challenging scenarios.

Rapid Decision-Making

Military leadership prioritizes the capacity to make swift decisions despite having incomplete information. This essential skill, particularly crucial in combat scenarios, is honed through rigorous training and hands-on experience.

As a platoon leader, I frequently faced the necessity of making rapid decisions during operations. The military's leadership training equipped me to swiftly gather pertinent information, formulate a decision, and fully commit to that choice.

Focus on Mission Accomplishment

The steadfast dedication to achieving mission objectives is a notable strength of military leadership. This clear sense of purpose fuels every action and decision.

Throughout my deployment in the Gulf War, this mission-driven mindset effectively navigated through confusion, ensuring the unit maintained its forward momentum despite various challenges and obstacles.

Development of Future Leaders

The military is exceptional at systematically cultivating future leaders. From the very beginning of a soldier's career, leadership skills are instilled, practiced, and rigorously assessed.

My personal journey through numerous leadership courses and roles serves as a testament to this structured approach to leader growth.

These strengths of military leadership benefitted me and my fellow soldiers immensely during our time in the armed forces. They fostered leaders who were decisive, resilient, ethical, and dedicated to mission accomplishment. However, as we will delve into in later chapters, transitioning to civilian leadership necessitates adapting these strengths to an entirely different environment.

Limitations and Potential Pitfalls

While the military's approach to leadership boasts numerous strengths, it also presents limitations and potential pitfalls, especially when utilized beyond military settings. Acknowledging these drawbacks is essential for anyone making the transition from military to civilian leadership.

Overdependence on Hierarchy

The military's rigid hierarchical structure can foster an excessive reliance on rank and position to establish authority. This can suppress initiative and cultivate a culture in which subordinates hesitate to express concerns or present alternative viewpoints.

During my initial experiences as a civilian leader, I often felt frustrated when team members did not instinctively defer to my decisions as they would have in the military setting. I had to adapt to the realization that, in the civilian world, authority frequently must be earned rather than simply assumed.

Inflexibility and Resistance to Change

The military's focus on standard operating procedures and established protocols, though essential in various contexts, can create inflexibility and a reluctance to embrace change. This rigidity can pose a considerable drawback in the fast-paced, ever-evolving landscape of civilian business.

I remember a time when my commitment to a fixed plan almost cost my team a crucial contract. It served as a wake-up call, illustrating that in the business realm, adaptability frequently outweighs strict compliance with procedure.

Overemphasis on Top-Down Communication

While effective communication is a hallmark of military leadership, there is frequently an excessive focus on top-down communication. This tendency can result in a deficiency of upward feedback, ultimately stifling innovation from lower ranks.

During my transition to civilian leadership, I had to intentionally focus on establishing avenues for bottom-up communication and fostering idea generation.

Difficulty Handling Ambiguity

Military operations typically demand clear, binary decisions. This requirement can pose challenges when transitioning to civilian business contexts, where ambiguity often clouds the best course of action.

In my early civilian leadership roles, I frequently grappled with this issue, often advocating for quick, decisive actions when a more thoughtful, exploratory approach would have been far more suitable.

Potential for Authoritarianism

The demand for unquestioning obedience in combat scenarios can occasionally result in a leadership style that leans toward excessive authoritarianism. This tendency frequently backfires in civilian environments, where collaboration and consensus-building hold significant importance.

I discovered this lesson the hard way when my directive approach fostered resentment and diminished productivity within my first civilian team.

Challenge in Managing Diverse Teams

While the military has made significant strides toward increasing diversity, civilian workplaces often showcase a variety of backgrounds, perspectives, and work styles that can be daunting for those used to the uniformity of military life.

Adapting to leading teams composed of individuals with diverse educational qualifications, work experiences, and cultural perspectives emerged as one of the most significant challenges during my transition into leadership.

Difficulty with Work-Life Balance

The military's demand for unwavering commitment can pose challenges for leaders transitioning to civilian environments, particularly in terms of establishing a healthy work-life balance. This often results in burnout or fosters unrealistic expectations among civilian workers.

I had to realize that anticipating my civilian team to exhibit the same level of dedication as my military units—available around the clock—was neither feasible nor effective.

Overemphasis on Toughness

The military's emphasis on mental and physical resilience, though essential in combat scenarios, can occasionally result in diminished empathy and comprehension in civilian environments. This disconnect can pose significant challenges in fostering employee well-being and maintaining a healthy work-life balance.

In my initial leadership positions in civilian settings, I found it difficult to recognize and address the personal needs and struggles of my team members. I eventually discovered that demonstrating compassion and adaptability frequently yielded superior long-term results compared to insisting on relentless toughness.

Difficulty with Ambiguous Success Metrics

In the military, success is typically well-defined—the mission is either accomplished, or it falls short. In contrast, success in the business world can be far more nuanced and focused on the long term. This difference can pose challenges for military leaders as they transition to environments where success is assessed in less tangible terms.

Early in my transition, I experienced considerable frustration due to the absence of clear "win" conditions in various business projects. Adapting to the process of setting and striving for more ambiguous, long-term objectives was a significant adjustment for me.

Potential for Micromanagement

The military's focus on meticulous attention to detail and oversight can often lead to micromanagement in civilian environments. This tendency can hinder creativity and dampen employee initiative.

I had to deliberately make an effort to step back and grant my team members greater autonomy, placing my trust in their skills rather than attempting to oversee every facet of their work.

Acknowledging these limitations and potential challenges is essential for military leaders transitioning to civilian positions. Recognizing these inclinations in myself marked the initial step in modifying my leadership approach to become more effective in a civilian setting.

Chapter 2
Early Missteps in Civilian Leadership

The Civilian Work Environment

Stepping into my first civilian leadership role felt akin to landing on an alien planet. The familiar structures and protocols of military life had vanished, replaced by an atmosphere that initially appeared disorganized and ineffective.

What struck me first was the physical environment. The uniformed personnel and strictly regimented spaces were nowhere to be seen. Instead, I was in an open-plan office filled with casually dressed employees. The lack of visible rank insignia was especially disconcerting—how was I supposed to discern who held authority?"

The work rhythm was also strikingly different. In the military, our days revolved around PT, formations, and clearly defined duty hours. In the civilian realm, I discovered a much more flexible approach to time. Some team members showed up early, while others arrived late. Lunch breaks were not taken collectively but were staggered throughout the day. The idea of an 'end of duty day' felt vague, as some employees stayed late while others departed promptly at 5 PM."

Decision-making processes presented another layer of culture shock. In the military, decisions typically flowed down from above and were executed without hesitation. However, in my new civilian role, I discovered that even relatively minor decisions often entailed lengthy discussions, committees, and consensus-building activities. What I perceived as straightforward issues that could be settled with a swift order frequently evolved into drawn-out debates."

The diversity within the civilian workplace represented a major shift. Although the military has made commendable progress in promoting diversity, the civilian sector showcased an even wider array of backgrounds, experiences, and viewpoints. I discovered that I was collaborating with individuals possessing significantly different educational histories, work experiences, and outlooks on life. This diversity, though ultimately a valuable asset, initially posed challenges in terms of management.

Communication styles in the civilian realm were also strikingly distinct. The straightforward, no-nonsense communication that I had been trained in during my military career frequently appeared blunt or even impolite in this new setting. I needed to adapt by softening my language and becoming more sensitive to the subtleties of office politics and interpersonal relationships.

One of the most profound differences lies in the essential nature of authority and motivation. In the military, my authority was intrinsically linked to my rank, and my unit's motivation stemmed from a collective sense of duty and mission. However, in the civilian landscape, I soon recognized that authority must be cultivated through demonstrated competence and interpersonal abilities, rather than simply granted by one's position. Motivation was influenced by a multifaceted blend of elements, including individual career aspirations, financial incentives, and overall job satisfaction.

This new environment necessitated a thorough reevaluation of my leadership approach. The skills and habits that had proven effective in the military were not only insufficient; in many instances, they were outright counterproductive. I recognized that a steep learning curve awaited me if I aimed to thrive in this unfamiliar realm.

Cultural Clashes and Misunderstandings

The shift from military to civilian leadership was filled with cultural clashes and misinterpretations. Much of this arose from the significant differences in norms, expectations, and communication styles inherent in each world.

One of my initial blunders took place in a team meeting during my first week at the job. Used to the military's method of delivering clear, direct orders, I presented a project plan in what I believed was a simple manner. Johnson, you will manage the market research. I expect it on my desk by Wednesday. Smith, you are responsible for the financial projections. I need those by Thursday. Any questions?"

The silence that ensued was overwhelming. I took it as acceptance and agreement—in the military, silence following orders typically indicated understanding and compliance. It was only later that I discovered my team perceived my approach as abrupt and authoritarian. They were accustomed to being solicited for input, engaging in discussions about deadlines, and enjoying greater autonomy in how they managed their responsibilities."

If you have seen the movie "A Few Good Men", there is a courtroom scene that relates to relates to the themes in this chapter about military vs. civilian leadership styles.

The dialogue between Lt. Kaffee and Col. Jessup underscores the significant contrasts between the military chain of command and the practice of questioning authority. Within the military framework, following orders without question is the norm, mirroring my initial approach to leadership. Yet, in civilian environments, this blind obedience can result in misunderstandings and foster resentment.

Similar to Lt. Kaffee, civilian employees frequently require an understanding of the rationale behind directives. They might challenge or inquire, not from a place of disrespect, but because they see it as essential for the effective performance of their responsibilities. This highlights the understanding that in civilian leadership, authority must be cultivated through demonstrated competence and effective communication, rather than merely assumed based on rank or position.

A further cultural clash emerged regarding the concept of punctuality. In the military, the phrase 'If you're not early, you're late' was a principle I adhered to. However, in my civilian position, I initially perceived team members arriving at 9:05 for a 9:00 meeting as disrespectful and lacking discipline. Over time, I came to realize that in numerous civilian workplaces, a few minutes of leeway was standard and did not reflect a deficiency in commitment or respect.

My methods for addressing performance issues also caused misunderstandings. Accustomed to the military's straightforward approach to confronting shortcomings, I once publicly critiqued a team member's work during a meeting. While I viewed this as clear and constructive feedback, it was seen as humiliating and disheartening by both the individual and the rest of the team. I had to recognize that in the civilian realm, discussions about performance were typically conducted privately and with greater consideration for individual feelings.

The notion of work-life balance presented yet another cultural clash. Familiar with the military's expectation of 24/7 availability, I initially found it challenging to understand and respect my team's boundaries between professional and personal life. My habit of sending emails late at night and anticipating immediate replies was perceived as intrusive and unreasonable.

My language also contributed to misunderstandings. Military jargon and acronyms that came naturally to me were perplexing or meaningless to my civilian team. My use of expressions like 'mission critical' or 'fall in line' frequently generated more confusion than clarity.

Possibly the most profound cultural clash revolved around the very nature of leadership. In the military, leadership often centered on having the right answers and making swift, decisive decisions. In my civilian role, I discovered that leadership leaned more towards asking the right questions, facilitating discussions, and fostering consensus. My early attempts to consistently provide answers and make unilateral decisions were frequently met with resistance and resentment.

These cultural clashes and misunderstandings proved frustrating and often demoralizing. Nevertheless, they also functioned as invaluable learning experiences, compelling me to reassess my leadership approach and cultivate new skills that were more aligned with the civilian environment.

Detailed Accounts of Leadership Failures

While the transition to civilian leadership was marked by many small missteps, there were a few significant leadership failures that stand out in my memory. These experiences, though painful at the time, proved to be valuable learning opportunities.

The Project Management Debacle

One of my most significant failures took place approximately three months into my new position. We were assigned the responsibility of launching a new product line, a venture that demanded collaboration across various departments. Relying on my military background, I treated this as if it were a military mission. I developed an elaborate plan that outlined specific tasks and deadlines for each team member, providing minimal room for flexibility or input.

As the project advanced, I began to observe rising tension and resentment within the team. Team members were missing deadlines, and the quality of the output was declining. Rather than tackling the root issues, I intensified my military-style tactics, implementing daily 'status report' meetings and publicly reprimanding those who were lagging behind.

The crisis reached its peak when two essential team members approached HR regarding transfers to different departments. It was at that moment I fully grasped the magnitude of my failure. My inflexible approach had suppressed creativity, demoralized the team, and fostered a fear-driven environment that was actively obstructing our progress.

This failure taught me the importance of flexibility, collaborative planning, and creating an environment where team members feel valued and heard.

The Motivation Misfire

Another significant failure occurred when I tried to motivate my team using techniques that had worked well in the military. Facing a tight deadline on a critical project, I decided to give a rousing speech reminiscent of those given before military operations.

I convened the team and launched into an impassioned speech about duty, sacrifice, and the significance of our mission. I emphasized the need to persevere through fatigue, exceed expectations, and do whatever was necessary to achieve our goals. I anticipated that this would spark enthusiasm within the team, prompting them to unite around our cause and dedicate themselves to extended hours and additional effort.

Rather than the response I hoped for, I was greeted with an uneasy silence and doubtful expressions. In the subsequent days, rather than seeing a boost in motivation, I observed a decline in both morale and productivity. Numerous team members appeared to retreat, opting to perform only the bare minimum instead of exerting themselves further.

A candid discussion with a trusted colleague was necessary for me to recognize my missteps. My military-style motivation, centered on duty and sacrifice, had been perceived as disconnected and manipulative within a civilian framework. Team members sensed that I was attempting to induce guilt to make them overextend themselves without appropriate compensation or acknowledgment."

This failure taught me that motivation in the civilian world is much more individual and often tied to personal growth, recognition, and tangible rewards rather than appeals to duty or mission.

The Feedback Fiasco

A third notable failure centered on my method of providing feedback. In the military, feedback was typically straightforward, prompt, and concentrated on correction. I adopted this same method in my civilian role, convinced that candid, unfiltered feedback was the most effective way to enhance performance.

This method culminated in a catastrophic performance review with one of my team leaders. By concentrating exclusively on areas needing improvement, I unleashed a barrage of criticisms while failing to recognize his strengths or accomplishments. I concluded the review with what I mistakenly believed was an inspiring challenge to 'shape up or ship out."

The result was disastrous. The team leader, who had once been a reliable performer, grew disengaged and bitter. His performance declined further, ultimately leading him to leave the company, citing my leadership as a major factor in his decision.

This failure taught me the importance of stable feedback, the need to recognize and reinforce positive performance, and the value of a more cooperative approach to performance improvement.

These failures, though difficult to experience, were vital in my development as a civilian leader. They highlighted the areas where my military leadership style was misaligned with civilian expectations and needs, pushing me to evolve and adapt my approach.

Employee Perspectives on Authoritarian Leadership

One of the most valued lessons in my change to civilian leadership came from actively seeking out and listening to employee perspectives on my leadership style. This feedback, though often difficult to hear, provided crucial insights into how my military-influenced, authoritarian approach was being received.

Anonymous Feedback Survey

About six months into my role, HR conducted an anonymous feedback survey about my leadership. The results were a wake-up call. Here are some of the comments that stood out:

From Command To Collaboration: A Journey In Modern Leadership

"It feels like we're in boot camp, not a creative marketing department." "I'm afraid to voice my opinions because they'll just be shot down." "The constant pressure and criticism are killing my motivation." "It's like working for a drill sergeant, not a team leader."

These comments made me realize that my leadership style, which I had seen as strong and decisive, was being perceived as overbearing and demotivating.

One-on-One Conversations

After seeing the survey results, I decided to have one-on-one conversations with team members to get more detailed feedback. These conversations were enlightening:

One team member said, "I appreciate that you're direct and clear about expectations, but it often feels like there's no room for discussion or alternative ideas. In our field, some of the best solutions come from collaborative brainstorming."

Another noted, "The military-style discipline can be motivating in small doses, but when it's constant, it becomes exhausting. We need some flexibility and understanding that we have lives outside of work."

A particularly insightful comment came from a senior team member: "In the military, your authority came with your rank. Here, you need to earn our trust and respect. That comes from listening to us, valuing our expertise, and creating an environment where we feel safe to take risks and occasionally fail."

Exit Interviews

Perhaps the most cruelly honest feedback came from exit interviews with employees who left the company. One departing employee said, "I've never worked in an environment where I felt so micromanaged and undervalued. Every decision had to go through you, and any deviation from your plan was treated like insubordination."

Another said, "The constant pressure to be 'mission-ready' was unsustainable. We're not soldiers, we're professionals with diverse skills and our own ways of working. The one-size-fits-all approach simply doesn't work in this environment."

Informal Feedback

Some of the most valuable insights came from informal conversations, often with employees who felt comfortable enough to be candid with me.

One team member pulled me aside after a particularly tense meeting and said, "You know, when you raise your voice and use that commanding tone, it doesn't motivate us. It just makes everyone shut down. We're not in the military where that kind of motivation works. Here, it just creates fear and resentment."

Another employee, after a few drinks at a company social event, confided, "We all respect your military background, but sometimes it feels like you're still fighting a war. We need a leader, not a commander."

These insights proved essential in illuminating the effects of my leadership style. They underscored the necessity for a more cooperative and adaptable approach that esteemed employee contributions and acknowledged the diverse motivations and work styles found within a civilian workplace.

The feedback further stressed the significance of emotional intelligence in civilian leadership—recognizing the necessity to be conscious of and regulate my own emotions while also being sensitive to the feelings and requirements of my team members.

This employee feedback played a pivotal role in my quest to refine my leadership style. It made me aware of the importance of harmonizing the strengths I carried from my military experience—such as clarity, decisiveness, and a results-oriented mindset—with new competencies better aligned with the civilian setting, such as cooperative decision-making, adaptability, and tailored motivation.

Analysis of Why Military Tactics Failed

Reflecting on my early failures and the feedback I received, I began to analyze why many of the leadership tactics that had served me well in the military were failing in my civilian role. This analysis was crucial in helping me understand what needed to change in my approach.

Difference in Power Dynamics

In the military, the chain of command is absolute. Orders flow from top to bottom, and disobedience can result in severe costs. In the civilian world, while there is still a hierarchy, power dynamics are much more fluid. Employees have the choice to disagree, to leave for other opportunities, or to simply disengage if they don't buy into the leadership approach.

My attempts to lead solely through positional authority proved ineffective, as in the civilian landscape, personal influence frequently holds greater significance than official rank.

Diverse Motivations

Military personnel are united by an unwavering sense of duty, deep-seated patriotism, and a shared mission. In the civilian world, however, motivations are vastly more diverse. Some employees are driven by ambitions for career advancement, while others seek intellectual challenges, work-life balance, or financial rewards.

My one-size-fits-all strategy for motivation, which relied on appeals to duty and mission accomplishment, ultimately failed to resonate with many team members who had differing primary motivators.

Emphasis on Individual Contribution

While the military places a high premium on teamwork, it also functions within a clearly defined rank structure, where individual responsibilities are typically rigidly outlined. Conversely, in many civilian workplaces, particularly those focused on knowledge work, the boundaries between roles tend to be more ambiguous, with a stronger emphasis on individual expertise and personal contributions.

My inclination to impose tasks and dictate methods without taking into account the unique strengths and preferences of each team member resulted in a significant underutilization of my team's varied skills and knowledge.

Different Risk Tolerance

In military operations, particularly during combat scenarios, errors can have fatal consequences. This reality demands a zero-tolerance policy for mistakes and a substantial amount of oversight. Conversely, in many civilian settings, especially within innovative or creative industries, a degree of risk-taking and failure is not only accepted but frequently celebrated as a vital component of the learning and growth process.

My low tolerance for mistakes and tendency to micromanage stifled creativity and innovation within my team.

Communication Style Mismatch

Military communication tends to be direct, concise, and top-down. While clarity is also valued in civilian communication, there's often a need for more diplomacy, more two-way dialogue, and more attention to emotional nuance.

My blunt, command-style communication often came across as harsh or insensitive in the civilian context, damaging relationships and team morale.

Flexibility vs. Rigid Structure

Military operations demand a significant level of organization and uniformity. Although organizations hold value in civilian workplaces as well, there is frequently a greater necessity for flexibility to adjust to swiftly evolving market dynamics or to cater to diverse individual work preferences.

My attempts to impose rigid structures and consistent procedures on all aspects of our work led to frustration and reduced agility in responding to business needs.

Different Concepts of Respect

In the military, respect is often tied to rank and is demonstrated through strict adherence to protocol and following orders. In civilian contexts, respect is more often earned through competence, emotional intelligence, and the ability to collaborate effectively.

My expectation of automatic respect due to my position, and my interpretation of questioning or disagreement as disrespect, created barriers between me and my team.

Pace of Decision Making

Military operations frequently demand swift, decisive actions taken with minimal information. Although such urgency can occasionally be required in the business world, numerous civilian settings thrive on more thoughtful, collaborative decision-making methods that promote inclusivity.

My tendency to make hasty, unilateral decisions without soliciting input or building consensus often resulted in pushback during implementation and overlooked chances for better solutions.

Work-Life Balance Expectations

The military typically requires a commitment level that often merges personal and professional spheres. In numerous civilian environments, however, there exists a strong expectation for more distinct boundaries between work obligations and personal time.

My insistence on constant availability and the expectation that work should take precedence over everything else conflicted with my team's desire for a healthier work-life balance, resulting in fatigue and frustration.

Different Approaches to Conflict Resolution

In the military, conflicts are often resolved through the chain of command. In civilian contexts, there's often an expectation of more diplomatic, collaborative approaches to resolving disagreements.

My directive approach to settling disputes failed to address underlying issues and sometimes escalated conflicts rather than resolving them.

Understanding these essential differences proved vital in my quest to transform my leadership style. It made me realize that successful leadership in a civilian environment demands a distinct array of skills and methodologies compared to what had previously propelled my success in the military.

Lessons Learned and Initial Steps Toward Change

Recognizing the failures of my military-style leadership in the civilian context was a chastening experience, but it also marked the beginning of my growth as a leader. Here are some of the key lessons I learned and the initial steps I took to change my approach:

Lesson: Authority must be earned, not assumed

Initial Step: I began to focus on building relationships and demonstrating competence rather than relying on my position for authority. I made a conscious effort to learn from my team members, acknowledging their expertise and experience.

Lesson: Motivation is individual

From Command To Collaboration: A Journey In Modern Leadership

Initial Step: I started having one-on-one conversations with team members to understand their personal goals and motivations. I then tried to align their work and my feedback with these individual motivators.

Lesson: Collaboration often yields better results than top-down directives

Initial Step: I began involving the team in decision-making processes. Instead of issuing orders, I started asking for input and facilitating discussions to reach consensus on important decisions.

Lesson: Flexibility is crucial in a dynamic business environment

Initial Step: I worked on becoming more adaptable in my approach. Instead of rigid plans, I started setting broad objectives and allowing the team more autonomy in how to achieve them.

Lesson: Communication needs to be two-way

Initial Step: I made a conscious effort to listen more and speak less. I implemented regular feedback sessions where I actively sought input from the team on my leadership and our processes.

Lesson: Mistakes can be learning opportunities

Initial Step: I began to view errors differently, focusing on what could be learned rather than just on correction. I started encouraging calculated risk-taking and innovation, making it clear that well-intentioned mistakes were part of the growth process.

Lesson: Work-life balance is important for long-term productivity and retention

Initial Step: I reevaluated our work schedules and communication norms. I stopped sending emails outside of work hours and began respecting personal time more conscientiously.

Lesson: Emotional intelligence is crucial in civilian leadership

Initial Step: I enrolled in an emotional intelligence course and began practicing techniques to better recognize and manage my own emotions and those of my team members.

Lesson: Different situations call for different leadership styles

Initial Step: I started studying various leadership models and practicing adapting my style to different situations and individuals, rather than using a one-size-fits-all approach.

Lesson: Trust is the foundation of effective civilian leadership

Initial Step: I began delegating more substantive responsibilities to team members, demonstrating trust in their abilities. I also became more transparent about my own challenges and decision-making processes.

These insights and early actions signified the onset of my evolution as a leader. They established a foundation for a more inclusive, adaptable, and emotionally aware leadership approach that would demonstrate significantly greater effectiveness in the civilian landscape.

The path was neither smooth nor swift. Breaking old habits proved challenging, and I faced numerous instances of frustration and regression. Nevertheless, with each incremental adjustment, I started to witness enhancements in team morale, productivity, and my overall job satisfaction.

One particularly memorable moment came about three months into my efforts to change. After a project meeting where I had consciously focused on facilitating discussion rather than dictating a plan, a team member approached me privately. "I don't know what's changed," they said, "but it feels like we're finally working with you, not for you. It makes a big difference."

Comments like these, along with gradual improvements in team performance and morale, reinforced that I was on the right track. They gave me the motivation to continue pushing myself to evolve as a leader.

From Command To Collaboration: A Journey In Modern Leadership

This realization marked a pivotal moment in my leadership journey. Rather than perceiving my military background as a handicap to overcome, I started to recognize it as a distinct perspective that, when thoughtfully adapted, could add considerable value to my role in civilian leadership.

The lessons I gleaned from my early missteps and the initial actions I undertook to transform my approach laid the groundwork for the leadership philosophy I would continue to cultivate—one that fused the most effective elements of my military training with fresh skills and methods more aligned with the civilian sector. This evolving strategy toward leadership would serve as the foundation for the achievements and insights I'll be sharing in the forthcoming chapters.

Chapter 3:
The Power of Asking

The Psychology of Asking vs. Telling

As I started to reevaluate my leadership style, I encountered a simple yet profound transformation: the effectiveness of asking rather than merely telling. This shift in communication was revolutionary, influencing not just the outcomes but also the entire dynamic of my interactions with my team.

The military had instilled in me a rigid 'command and control' mindset, where orders were delivered without room for discussion. However, in the civilian landscape, I realized that posing questions created new opportunities and levels of engagement that straightforward commands could never achieve.

Psychologically, there's a significant difference between being told what to do and being asked for input:

1. Autonomy: When asked, people feel a sense of control over their work, which is a key motivator.

2. Cognitive Engagement: Questions stimulate thinking, while orders can shut it down.

3. Ownership: People are more committed to ideas they help create.

4. Respect: Asking demonstrates that you value the other person's knowledge and opinion.

5. Trust: It shows you trust your team's judgment and expertise.

I recall a crucial moment when this transformation took hold. We were up against a challenging deadline for a project, and my initial reaction was to start barking orders. However, I took a moment to reflect and instead asked, "What do you think is the best way to tackle this?"

The silence that followed felt awkward at first, but soon, ideas began to emerge. Team members started to build on one another's suggestions, and the solution we ultimately crafted surpassed anything I could have imagined alone.

This experience enlightened me to the fact that asking questions isn't an indication of weakness or uncertainty. On the contrary, it's a potent tool for tapping into the collective intelligence of a team, fostering a culture rich in collaboration and innovation.

Benefits of an Inquisitive Leadership Style

As I continued to incorporate more questioning into my leadership style, I began to notice a multitude of benefits:

1. Enhanced Problem-Solving: By posing questions, I unlocked the vast reservoir of knowledge and experiences within my team. Challenges that once appeared insurmountable often yielded groundbreaking solutions when tackled collaboratively.

2. Increased Employee Engagement: When team members sensed that their ideas held weight, they became more emotionally invested in their tasks. I observed a noticeable uptick in proactive behaviors and initiative-taking across the board.

3. Better Decision-Making: Gathering multiple perspectives through questioning led to more informed and robust decisions.

4. Improved Learning Culture: Asking questions modeled curiosity and continuous learning, encouraging team members to do the same.

5. Stronger Relationships: The act of asking and listening built trust and rapport within the team.

6. Greater Adaptability: An inquisitive approach made us more responsive to changes, as we were constantly seeking to understand our environment.

7. Empowered Employees: By asking instead of telling, I helped team members develop their own problem-solving skills.

One specific project remains etched in my memory as a powerful example of these advantages. We were challenged with creating a new product line, a task that would have previously driven me to craft and impose a rigid plan. This time, however, I began by asking questions: "What opportunities do we identify in the market? Which strengths can we capitalize on? What potential risks should we consider?"

The resulting dialogue was dynamic and fruitful. Team members from various departments contributed their distinctive perspectives. Marketing uncovered overlooked customer needs, operations emphasized our production capabilities, and finance shared critical insights on cost factors.

The final product concept emerged as both innovative and comprehensive, meeting market demands while aligning with our strengths. More significantly, the team felt invigorated and dedicated to ensuring its success like I had never witnessed before.

This experience solidified my belief that the advantages of an inquisitive leadership style reach far beyond simply generating better ideas; it reshapes the entire workplace culture and enhances the employee experience.

Techniques for Effective Questioning

As I began to harness the power of inquiry, it became clear to me that not all questions hold the same weight. Mastering the art of effective questioning is a skill that demands ongoing practice and careful refinement. Below are some techniques I discovered to be especially beneficial:

1. Open-Ended Questions: Rather than sticking to simple yes/no inquiries, I discovered the power of asking questions that encourage deeper responses. For instance, instead of saying, "Do you think this approach will work?" I learned to ask, "What are your thoughts on this approach?"

2. Clarifying Questions: These types of questions are crucial for ensuring comprehension and demonstrate that I am actively engaged in the conversation. Phrases like, "Can you elaborate on...?" or "What do you mean when you say...?" has proven to be effective.

3. Probing Questions: These dig deeper into an issue. "What factors led you to that conclusion?" or "How might this impact our other initiatives?"

4. Hypothetical Questions: These encourage creative thinking. "What if we approached this from a completely different angle?"

5. Reflective Questions: These promote self-analysis and learning. "Looking back, what would you do differently?"

6. Circular Questions: These explore relationships and systemic impacts. "How do you think this decision might affect our partners?"

7. Scale Questions: These help quantify subjective experiences. "On a scale of 1-10, how confident are you about this approach?"

I discovered that preparing key questions ahead of meetings was beneficial, yet I also needed to stay adaptable and pose follow-up inquiries depending on the answers I received.

One particularly effective technique was the "Five Whys" method. Whenever I encountered a problem, I would ask "Why?" five times to uncover the root cause. For example, when addressing ongoing project delays:

1. Why are we consistently missing deadlines? "Because we're often waiting on input from other departments."

2. Why are we waiting on other departments? "Because they're not aware of our timelines."

3. Why aren't they aware of our timelines? "Because we don't have a system for sharing project schedules across departments."

4. Why don't we have such a system? "Because we've always operated in silos."

5. Why have we operated in silos? "Because we've never prioritized cross-departmental collaboration."

This approach frequently resulted in insights that might have slipped through the cracks with a more cursory examination.

Another impactful questioning technique I embraced was appreciative inquiry. Rather than concentrating on the issues at hand, I began to ask questions regarding what was functioning effectively and how we could amplify those successes. This optimistic perspective invigorated the team and frequently sparked innovative solutions.

Case Studies: Transformations Through Asking

As I continued to refine my questioning techniques, I witnessed several remarkable transformations within our organization. Here are a few case studies that highlight the power of an inquisitive leadership approach:

Case Study 1: The Underperforming Team Member

John had been facing difficulties with his performance for several months. In the past, I would have responded by reprimanding him or placing him on a performance improvement plan. However, this time,

From Command To Collaboration: A Journey In Modern Leadership

I chose to sit down with him and ask, "Which aspects of your job do you find most challenging?" and "How do you believe your strengths could be leveraged more effectively?"

Through our discussion, I learned that John thrived in data analysis but had difficulties with client presentations. We revamped his role to emphasize his strengths and offered specialized training for his challenging areas. Within just three months, John transformed into one of our top performers.

Case Study 2: The Interdepartmental Conflict

Tension had been simmering between our sales and product development teams for quite some time. Instead of dictating a solution, I decided to unite both teams and posed the questions, "What does success look like for each of your departments?" and "How can we bring these visions into alignment?"

This approach sparked a constructive dialogue in which both teams gained insights into each other's challenges and priorities. As a result, they collaborated to create a new process that enhanced both product quality and sales effectiveness.

Case Study 3: The Innovation Challenge

Our company was steadily losing market share and desperately needed innovative ideas. Rather than turning to costly consultants, I decided to engage our entire staff with a series of thought-provoking questions: "If you could change one thing about our products, what would it be?" and "Which customer needs are we currently failing to meet?"

The feedback we received was nothing short of remarkable. We amassed hundreds of suggestions, many originating from employees in departments that typically didn't participate in product development. A standout idea from a junior accountant resulted in a new product feature that ultimately became our most significant market differentiator.

These examples illustrated that the art of asking questions transcends mere information gathering. It has the potential to unlock hidden talent, resolve conflicts, and spur innovation in ways that top-down directives simply cannot achieve.

Overcoming Resistance to a Questioning Approach

While the benefits of an inquisitive leadership style were clear, I encountered resistance both from myself and from others as I implemented this new approach. Here's how I addressed some common challenges:

1. Personal Discomfort: At first, I felt exposed when I chose to ask questions instead of simply providing answers. I had to constantly remind myself that real strength comes from tapping into the collective wisdom of the team rather than relying solely on my own knowledge.

2. Team Expectations: Some members of the team were initially perplexed or irritated when I solicited their input instead of issuing commands. I took the time to clarify the rationale behind my new approach and consistently demonstrated that I genuinely valued their insights.

3. Time Concerns: There was a prevailing belief that asking questions and engaging in discussions consumed too much time. I addressed this concern by illustrating how this initial investment of time ultimately led to superior solutions and quicker execution.

4. Fear of Appearing Incompetent: Some team members were hesitant to answer questions, fearing they might give the "wrong" answer. I worked to create a safe environment where all ideas were welcomed and explored.

5. Resistance to Change: A few long-time employees were resistant to this new leadership style. I worked with them individually, demonstrating the benefits and addressing their specific concerns.

Balancing Inquiry and Advocacy

As I began to embrace the power of asking, I recognized the critical need to balance inquiry (the act of asking questions) with advocacy (voicing my own perspectives). Excessive inquiry without providing any clear direction could result in paralysis by analysis, while an overemphasis on advocacy would cause me to fall back into my previous command-and-control mentality.

I developed a framework for myself:

1. Start with Inquiry: Begin discussions by asking open-ended questions to gather information and perspectives.

2. Encourage Diverse Viewpoints: Actively seek out different opinions, especially from quieter team members.

3. Summarize and Clarify: Periodically summarize what I've heard to ensure understanding.

4. Share My Perspective: After hearing from others, I would share my own thoughts, clearly stating my reasoning.

5. Invite Challenge: Encourage the team to question and challenge my views.

6. Collaborative Decision-Making: Work together to synthesize the various perspectives into a decision or action plan.

This balanced strategy enabled me to offer guidance and make informed decisions when required, all while harnessing the collective wisdom of the team.

Practical Exercises in the Art of Asking

To help embed this new leadership style, I developed several exercises for myself and my team:

1. The Question-Only Meeting: I occasionally held meetings where only questions could be asked – no statements allowed. This forced us to explore issues deeply before jumping to solutions.

2. The Curiosity Journal: I kept a journal of insightful questions I encountered, reflecting on why they were effective.

3. The Role Reversal: In one-on-ones, I sometimes had team members ask me questions about a project or decision, helping them develop their own questioning skills.

4. The Question Relay: In team meetings, each person had to build on the previous question asked before offering their own insights.

5. The "I Don't Know" Challenge: I encouraged team members (and myself) to become comfortable saying "I don't know, but I'll find out," rather than bluffing or avoiding difficult questions.

These exercises facilitated the transformation of powerful questioning from a mere technique into an ingrained habit, fundamentally reshaping our communication and problem-solving methods as a cohesive team.

In conclusion, embracing the power of inquiry represented a pivotal moment in my leadership journey. It enabled me to unlock the full potential of my team, cultivate a culture of curiosity and innovation, and ultimately drive superior results. Although it necessitated overcoming initial discomfort and resistance, the advantages significantly outweighed the challenges faced. As we transition into the next chapter, we will examine how this inquisitive approach

From Command To Collaboration: A Journey In Modern Leadership

established the foundation for a new model of leadership—leading from within.

Chapter 4:
Leading from Within

The "Helicopter Formation" Model in Depth

As I progressed in refining my leadership style, I began to contemplate a striking metaphor from my military experiences: the helicopter formation. In military aviation, when a fleet of helicopters transports a Commanding General, the General's helicopter is customarily positioned third in line, rather than leading from the front or lagging at the back. This unique positioning resonated with me as a profound mctaphor for effective leadership in the civilian sector.

The "Helicopter Formation" model of leadership can be broken down as follows:

Not Leading from the Front: By choosing not to occupy the front position, a leader encourages others to step up, promoting initiative and nurturing the next generation of leaders. In a business context, this approach translates to empowering team members to spearhead projects or initiatives.

Avoiding the Back: Positioning oneself at the rear can create a disconnect from the realities faced on the ground. In the realm of business, this often results in losing sight of daily operations or the actual needs of customers.

Positioned in the Middle: From this central location, the leader can effectively observe both the front and rear, offering guidance and support as necessary. In an organizational setting, this enables a leader to maintain connections across all levels of the company.

This model resonated deeply with me because it addressed many challenges I encountered while transitioning from military to civilian leadership. It offered a robust framework for sustaining effective leadership while steering clear of the traps associated with an excessively authoritarian or aloof style.

Leading from within allows a leader to:

1. Empower others by giving them opportunities to take the lead

2. Stay connected to both strategic and operational aspects of the business

3. Provide support and guidance without micromanaging

4. Foster a more collaborative and innovative environment

5. Develop the next generation of leaders within the organization

As I started to put this model into practice, I observed a remarkable transformation in team dynamics. Team members began to adopt a more proactive stance, assuming ownership of their projects and decision-making processes. Simultaneously, I found myself increasingly aligned with both the overarching strategic objectives and the daily challenges my team encountered.

Empowering Others to Lead

One of the most pivotal elements of the "Helicopter Formation" model is the strong focus on empowering others to take the lead. This represented a substantial departure from my previous top-down strategy, but I swiftly recognized its potential to revolutionize our team's performance and boost morale. I began by pinpointing opportunities for team members to assume leadership roles on various projects or initiatives. Rather than being the sole presenter to senior management or clients, I started selecting team members for these important roles. For instance, when we needed to present a new strategy to the board, I chose not to take the stage myself. Instead, I mentored Sarah, a promising team member, to deliver the presentation. This not only provided Sarah with invaluable experience but also highlighted the depth of talent within our team to the board.

To ensure this empowerment was effective, I discovered that I needed to:

1. Provide Clear Objectives: While giving team members the freedom to lead, I made sure they understood the overall goals and constraints of the project.

2. Offer Support and Resources: I made it clear that while they were leading, I was available to provide guidance and resources as needed.

3. Allow for Mistakes: I had to resist the urge to step in at the first sign of trouble. Allowing team members to work through challenges was crucial for their development.

4. Recognize and Celebrate Success: When team members succeeded in their leadership roles, I made sure to recognize and celebrate their achievements.

5. Provide Constructive Feedback: After each leadership opportunity, I would sit down with the team member to discuss what went well and areas for improvement.

This approach did present its fair share of challenges. Some team members were initially reluctant to embrace leadership roles, while others exhibited an overzealous eagerness that necessitated guidance on effective collaborative leadership. Striking the right balance required both patience and continuous communication.

Nevertheless, the outcomes were nothing short of remarkable. Team members experienced significant growth in both confidence and capability. They began to perceive themselves not merely as task executors but as vital contributors to the company's overall success. This transformation in perspective sparked a wave of increased innovation, as team members felt empowered to propose and implement fresh ideas.

Facilitating Learning Through Experience

A fundamental component of leading from within involves generating opportunities for team members to engage in learning through hands-

From Command To Collaboration: A Journey In Modern Leadership

on experience. This method represented a major shift from the more authoritative style I had previously practiced in the military.

I began to see my role less as a commander giving orders, and more as a facilitator of learning experiences. Here's how I implemented this:

1. Stretch Assignments: I started assigning team members to projects that were slightly beyond their current capabilities. This challenged them to grow and develop new skills.

2. Guided Problem-Solving: When team members came to me with problems, instead of providing solutions, I asked guiding questions to help them find answers themselves.

3. Reflection Sessions: After key projects or decisions, I instituted "reflection sessions" where we would discuss what went well, what didn't, and what we learned.

4. Cross-Functional Experiences: I encouraged team members to work on projects outside their usual domains, fostering a broader understanding of the business.

5. Mentoring Programs: I set up a mentoring program where more experienced team members could guide and support newer ones.

One particularly impactful strategy I implemented was the "learning journal." I encouraged team members to maintain a journal documenting their experiences, insights, and inquiries as they embraced new responsibilities. We then utilized these journals as a foundation for our one-on-one discussions, centering on their growth and development.

This method of fostering learning came with its own set of challenges. It frequently required more time than merely instructing individuals on what to do, and there were occasions when errors occurred. However, the long-term advantages regarding team capability and engagement far surpassed these temporary inefficiencies.

I recall a specific situation where this method yielded significant results. We had an important client presentation, and I entrusted it to

Paul, a gifted but inexperienced team member. I collaborated with him on the preparation, but during the presentation, he faced challenging questions from the client.

My instinct urged me to intervene and take control, but I held back. Instead, I observed as Paul regrouped, tackled the client's concerns, and ultimately secured their approval. In our reflection session afterward, Paul expressed that this experience taught him more about client management than any formal training session ever could.

Providing Direction While Fostering Independence

One of the most intricate balances I needed to achieve in adopting the "leading from within" approach was delivering explicit direction while simultaneously nurturing autonomy and initiative among my team. This called for a profound transformation in how I articulated goals and expectations.

I developed a framework I called "Clarity, Context, and Choice":

1. **Clarity:** I made sure to clearly communicate the overall objectives and key performance indicators. This provided a clear destination for the team.

2. **Context:** I shared the broader strategic context of our work. Understanding how their efforts fit into the bigger picture helped team members make better decisions.

3. **Choice:** Within the framework of our objectives and strategy, I gave team members the freedom to choose how to achieve the goals.

This approach proved especially successful during a significant reorganization project we initiated. Rather than imposing directives on how each department should reshape itself, I articulated our overarching goals—enhanced efficiency and improved customer responsiveness—along with the larger context of evolving industry dynamics and shifting customer expectations.

Following this, I encouraged each department head to craft their own reorganization strategy. The outcomes were remarkable. Not only did we meet our efficiency targets, but we also witnessed the emergence of innovative structures that were far more aligned with each department's specific challenges than anything I could have conceived on my own.

Implementing this approach required me to:

1. Improve my communication skills to ensure clarity without being overly prescriptive

2. Develop greater trust in my team's capabilities

3. Be comfortable with different approaches to achieving goals

4. Focus on outcomes rather than processes

5. Provide support and resources without taking over

It wasn't always a walk in the park. There were moments when I noticed teams venturing down paths that raised my concerns. It required a great deal of self-control to pose questions and provide guidance instead of simply steering them back on track. However, time and again, I discovered that by balancing direction with the encouragement of independence, we not only reached more effective solutions but also cultivated a more engaged and self-assured team.

Case Studies Across Industries

As I honed my "leading from within" methodology, I started observing that similar concepts were being effectively implemented across a range of industries. Below are several case studies that showcase the remarkable impact of this leadership model:

Case Study 1: Tech Startup

A rapidly expanding tech startup faced challenges in preserving its innovative spirit during its growth phase. The CEO, Sarah, adopted a "leading from within" strategy. She ceased participating in all product development meetings and instead empowered her team leaders to spearhead innovation. She established clear objectives (such as staying ahead of market trends) and provided the necessary context (regarding evolving customer needs), granting her teams the autonomy to pursue new ideas.

The outcome was a surge of creativity. In the absence of the CEO, team members felt freer to suggest and experiment with bold concepts. One such idea resulted in a groundbreaking product that ultimately doubled the company's market share.

Case Study 2: Manufacturing Company

A conventional manufacturing firm was grappling with heightened competition from international markets. The newly appointed COO, John, recognized that frontline workers frequently possessed the most valuable insights for enhancing efficiency but were seldom included in discussions.

He launched a "shop floor leadership" initiative, where he and other executives engaged directly with frontline employees. This approach enabled them to offer strategic guidance while gaining firsthand knowledge of daily challenges. Additionally, they introduced a system that empowered workers to propose and spearhead improvement initiatives.

Within a year, the company experienced a remarkable 20% boost in productivity, coupled with a notable enhancement in employee satisfaction and retention.

Case Study 3: Healthcare Provider

A sizable hospital faced significant challenges with its patient satisfaction ratings. The Chief Nursing Officer, Maria, recognized that nurses, who had the most direct interactions with patients, often felt ineffective in their ability to enhance the overall patient experience.

To address this, she launched a program empowering each nursing unit to design and implement their own patient experience initiatives.

While she provided training on best practices for patient experience and established clear success metrics, she also encouraged each unit to create strategies tailored to their specific patient demographics.

As a result, the hospital saw the emergence of a variety of innovative programs customized for different departments, ranging from enhanced communication tools in the ICU to individualized care plans in the oncology unit. Consequently, patient satisfaction scores surged, and nurse engagement levels skyrocketed.

These case studies illustrate how the principles of leading from within can be effectively leveraged across various industries and organizational cultures.

Challenges and Solutions in Implementation

Although the advantages of leading from within were evident, adopting this approach presented its own unique challenges. Below are some of the primary hurdles I faced and the strategies I devised to overcome them:

Challenge 1: Resistance to Empowerment

A number of team members expressed discomfort with the heightened responsibilities and expanded decision-making authority. They were used to following explicit orders and felt hesitant about taking the initiative.

Solution: I introduced a phased empowerment strategy. We began with less critical decisions and manageable projects, gradually broadening the scope as team members gained confidence. Additionally, I offered coaching and resources to assist them in honing their decision-making abilities.

Challenge 2: Maintaining Accountability

As leadership became more distributed, it became increasingly challenging to uphold clear accountability for results.

Solution: I created a structured system for goal-setting combined with consistent check-ins. We implemented OKRs (Objectives and Key Results) to guarantee that each individual comprehended their roles and how their contributions aligned with our overarching objectives.

Challenge 3: Balancing Freedom and Guidance

Certain projects stumbled due to insufficient guidance for team members, while in other cases, I found myself resorting to micromanagement.

Solution: I developed a "scaling involvement" framework. For every project, we would openly discuss and mutually agree on my level of engagement, making adjustments as needed throughout the project's lifecycle.

Challenge 4: Developing New Leadership Skills

Leading from within demanded a distinct skill set compared to my former command-and-control approach. I faced challenges in determining when to intervene and when to allow others to take the lead.

Solution: I committed to executive coaching and leadership development initiatives that emphasized collaborative leadership methodologies. Additionally, I established a peer support network with fellow leaders who were also navigating similar transitions.

Challenge 5: Organizational Culture Clash

The larger organization continued to function in a more conventional, hierarchical fashion, which at times conflicted with our team's innovative approach.

Solution: We took on the role of champions for our leadership style within the greater organization. I collaborated with HR to revise performance metrics and incentive systems, ensuring they were more in harmony with our collaborative methods. Additionally, we actively promoted our achievements, showcasing the advantages of our approach.

From Command To Collaboration: A Journey In Modern Leadership

By directly addressing these obstacles and crafting strategic solutions, we successfully implemented and maintained a "leading from within" framework.

Measuring Success in Collaborative Leadership

As we shifted toward a more collaborative leadership model, it became clear that our existing methods of measuring success needed a complete overhaul. Traditional metrics that emphasized individual achievements and top-down directives simply couldn't capture the nuances of our new approach. Here's how we redefined success to align with our evolving leadership style:

1. Team Performance Metrics:

Rather than concentrating only on individual accomplishments, we established new metrics centered around team performance. These metrics encompassed elements such as project completion rates, innovation indicators (tracking the number of new ideas successfully implemented), and evaluations of cross-functional collaboration effectiveness.

2. Employee Engagement Surveys:

We introduced consistent pulse surveys aimed at gauging employee engagement, overall satisfaction, and their perceived level of empowerment. We placed special emphasis on feedback regarding autonomy, mastery, and a sense of purpose.

3. Leadership Development Metrics:

We monitored the count of employees stepping into leadership roles for various projects and initiatives, closely observing their success rates. Additionally, we assessed the diversity within our pool of emerging leaders.

4. Decision Quality and Speed:

We established a framework to assess the quality of decisions made across different tiers of the organization, alongside evaluating the efficiency and speed of our decision-making processes.

5. Innovation Metrics:

We monitored not only the volume of new ideas conceived but also closely analyzed their execution rate and the tangible effects they had on the business.

6. Customer Satisfaction:

We theorized that giving employees greater empowerment would translate into improved customer outcomes. To validate this, we meticulously tracked customer satisfaction scores and analyzed feedback in detail.

7. Adaptability Metrics:

We devised methods to assess how effectively our organization could adapt to change, focusing on the time it took to roll out new initiatives and the success rates of our change programs.

8. Financial Performance:

Ultimately, we needed to prove that our new leadership strategy was positively impacting the bottom line. While we continued to monitor traditional financial metrics, we also focused on longer-term indicators that pointed to sustainable growth.

Rolling out these new success measures required full buy-in from the entire organization, including our Board of Directors. It was a journey of education and gradual adaptation, but over time, these metrics revealed a much deeper understanding of our organizational health and the effects of our collaborative leadership approach.

By the end of our first year, fully embracing the "leading from within" model, we experienced significant improvements across the majority of these metrics. Employee engagement scores rose by 35%, we doubled the number of innovative ideas implemented compared to the previous year, and our customer satisfaction scores jumped by 20%. Most promisingly, these advancements were mirrored in our financial performance, with revenue growth accelerating and profitability on the rise.

From Command To Collaboration: A Journey In Modern Leadership

These outcomes solidified the value of our new leadership strategy and laid the groundwork for its expansion throughout the organization. As we move forward, we'll delve into how this collaborative leadership style sets the foundation for rethinking our approach to innovation and creative problem-solving.

Chapter 5:
Rethinking "Outside the Box"

The Limitations of Traditional Brainstorming

As our leadership approach continued to evolve, I started to see that our methods for fostering innovation and tackling problems also required a shift. The old directive to simply "think outside the box," along with traditional brainstorming sessions, was no longer delivering the necessary results in our fast-paced business landscape.

The limitations of the "think outside the box" approach became increasingly apparent:

1. Lack of Direction: Telling people to think outside the box often left them feeling lost, without a clear starting point or framework for their ideas.

2. Pressure to be Revolutionary: The phrase could create anxiety, with team members feeling that only completely novel, groundbreaking ideas were valuable.

3. Disconnect from Reality: Truly "outside the box" ideas were often impractical or irrelevant to our actual business challenges.

4. Cognitive Overload: The vast, undefined space of "outside the box" could be overwhelming, leading to mental blocks rather than creativity.

Similarly, traditional brainstorming sessions had their own set of problems:

1. Dominance of Loud Voices: Often, the most outspoken team members would dominate, drowning out quieter voices.

2. Groupthink: The social dynamics of brainstorming could lead to convergent thinking rather than true diversity of ideas.

3. Lack of Deep Thinking: The rapid-fire nature of brainstorming often produced shallow ideas rather than well-considered solutions.

4. Premature Judgment: Despite rules against criticism, there was often subtle judgment of ideas, stifling creativity.

I vividly recall one exceptionally exasperating brainstorming session in which we aimed to generate fresh product concepts. After an hour had passed, we ended up with a whiteboard cluttered with outrageous, impractical ideas and scarcely any valuable insights. It became evident that a new strategy was essential.

This epiphany inspired me to create what I refer to as the "Expanding Circles" method, which we will delve into in the next section.

The "Expanding Circles" Method: A Detailed Guide

The "Expanding Circles" method emerged from the necessity for a more organized yet adaptable approach to innovation and problem-solving. Below is a comprehensive guide to this methodology:

Step 1: Define the Core

Begin by explicitly outlining the existing situation or challenge. This will serve as the focal point of your circle. For instance, if your goal is to enhance a product, the center would represent the existing iteration of that product.

Step 2: Create the First Circle

Encircle the central concept. This initial circle is where ideas that are directly linked to, or are requiring minor enhancements, to the existing situation. Typically, these are the most feasible and straightforward ideas to put into action.

Step 3: Add Outer Circles

Keep expanding the circles, with each additional one symbolizing concepts that are increasingly distanced from the center. The outer circles are where bolder, more innovative ideas can take shape.

Step 4: Fill the Circles

Invite team members to contribute ideas to every circle. Urge them to engage with all levels, not merely the outer ones. This approach fosters a balance between practical, incremental enhancements and more groundbreaking concepts.

Step 5: Connect Ideas

Seek out relationships among the ideas within various circles. Frequently, the most impactful innovations arise from the fusion of small adjustments with bolder concepts.

Step 6: Evaluate and Refine

Assess the ideas based on feasibility, potential impact, and alignment with goals. Refine the most promising concepts.

Here's an example of how we used this method to improve our customer service process:

Core: Current customer service system

Circle 1: Ideas like "Extend service hours" and "Add chat support."

Circle 2: "AI-powered chatbot," "Customer self-service portal."

Circle 3: "Predictive issue resolution," "VR-based product support."

Outer Circle: "Embedded AI in products for automatic issue reporting and resolution."

Utilizing this approach enabled us to produce a spectrum of ideas, spanning from quick, actionable enhancements to visionary, long-term innovations. The method's visual aspect also allowed team members to recognize how diverse ideas could interlink and reinforce one another.

Facilitating "Expanding Circles" Sessions

Effectively easing an "Expanding Circles" session is vital to its success. Here are some key strategies I developed:

From Command To Collaboration: A Journey In Modern Leadership

1. Set the Stage:

Begin by clearly explaining the method and its purpose. Emphasize that all ideas are valuable, whether they're in the inner or outer circles.

2. Provide Clear Parameters:

Define the core problem or situation clearly. Establish any constraints or criteria that solutions need to meet.

3. Encourage Diverse Thinking:

Prompt participants to consider different perspectives. For example, "How would a customer see this?" or "What would this look like in 10 years?"

4. Manage Time Effectively:

Allocate specific time for each circle. This prevents getting stuck on one type of idea and ensures a balance of incremental and radical thinking.

5. Foster a Safe Environment:

Reinforce that this is a judgment-free zone. All ideas should be recorded without criticism.

6. Encourage Building on Ideas:

Prompt participants to connect and combine ideas from different circles.

7. Use Visual Aids:

Whether using a physical whiteboard or digital tool, make sure the circles and ideas are visually represented.

8. Facilitate, Don't Direct:

Your role is to guide the process, not to generate or evaluate ideas. Ask questions to prompt deeper thinking or clarification.

9. End with Next Steps:

Wrap up the session by pinpointing the most promising ideas and detailing the next steps for assessment and execution.

Through my experience, I discovered that these sessions yielded their best results when limited to 60-90 minutes, featuring a varied mix of 6-8 participants. Additionally, supplying preparatory work, including relevant data or customer feedback, proved invaluable in enriching the ideation process.

Case Studies in Structured Innovation

The "Expanding Circles" method proved to be a multipurpose tool across various challenges and industries. Here are a few case studies that prove its effectiveness:

Case Study 1: Product Innovation in Tech

A software company faced challenges in standing out its project management tool amid a saturated marketplace. By employing the Expanding Circles method, they cultivated a variety of ideas, spanning from subtle UI enhancements to the incorporation of cutting-edge technologies.

Core: Current project management tool

Circle 1: Improved UI, better reporting features

Circle 2: AI-powered task prioritization, integrated time tracking

Circle 3: VR-based team collaboration spaces

Outer Circle: Predictive project outcomes based on vast cross-industry data

The company swiftly put the UI enhancements into action, commenced the development of AI capabilities, and initiated research and development on predictive outcomes technology. This layered strategy enabled them to implement quick upgrades while simultaneously striving for a genuinely groundbreaking long-term solution.

Case Study 2: Supply Chain Optimization in Manufacturing

A manufacturing firm recognized the necessity to enhance its supply chain resilience following disturbances triggered by global events. The Expanding Circles workshop generated a diverse array of solutions:

Core: Current supply chain model

Circle 1: Diversify suppliers, increase safety stock

Circle 2: Implement advanced forecasting algorithms and develop modular product designs for component flexibility

Circle 3: 3D printing of certain components, local micro-factories

Outer Circle: Fully autonomous, AI-driven supply chain with predictive disruption management

The company swiftly executed a blend of concepts drawn from the initial two circles, simultaneously launching pilot projects focused on 3D printing and localized production. The concept from the outer circle evolved into a strategic initiative for the long term.

Case Study 3: Customer Experience in Retail

A retail chain sought to transform the in-store shopping experience to effectively compete with the growing dominance of e-commerce. Their Expanding Circles session generated a variety of innovative ideas:

Core: Current in-store experience

Circle 1: Improved store layout, staff training in customer service

Circle 2: Mobile app for in-store navigation and instant product information

Circle 3: AR product visualization, VR home try-on stations

Outer Circle: Fully personalized shopping experiences driven by AI and biometric data

The retailer swiftly executed the concepts from the initial two circles across all locations, tested the AR/VR innovations in flagship stores, and initiated research into crafting a personalized shopping journey for future rollout.

These case studies illustrate how the Expanding Circles method can produce a wide spectrum of ideas, ranging from immediately implementable to far-reaching visionary concepts. This approach empowers organizations to enhance their current operations while simultaneously strategizing for future innovation.

Adapting the Method for Different Contexts

Although the foundational concepts of the Expanding Circles method stayed the same, I discovered that it could be tailored to fit various contexts and challenges effectively. Below are some adaptations we created:

1. Time-Based Circles:

Rather than merely illustrating a conceptual distance from the central idea, the circles now embodied various time frames: immediate, short-term, medium-term, and long-term solutions. This approach proved especially beneficial during strategic planning discussions.

2. Stakeholder Circles:

Each circle symbolizes a distinct stakeholder group (such as customers, employees, shareholders, and the community). This framework ensured that the proposed solutions took into account a variety of perspectives.

3. Resource Circles:

The circles illustrated varying degrees of resource allocation necessary. This approach proved advantageous for organizations facing resource constraints, facilitating a balance between quick wins and more daring initiatives.

4. Risk Circles:

The innermost circles signified ideas with minimal risk, while the level of risk escalated as you progressed outward. This framework proved beneficial for organizations with a conservative approach or those operating in highly regulated sectors.

5. Digital Adaptation:

We developed a digital adaptation of the tool specifically designed for remote teams, leveraging collaborative software that facilitated real-time sharing and clustering of ideas.

6. Continuous Circles:

To foster continuous innovation, we established a digital "idea bank" designed as expanding circles, enabling employees to contribute their ideas whenever they wanted.

These modifications empowered the method to be utilized effectively across various departments, spanning from product development to human resources and accommodating organizations of all sizes, from startups to large corporations.

Complementary Creativity Techniques

Although the Expanding Circles method emerged as our main instrument for organized innovation, we discovered that merging it with additional creativity techniques could significantly boost its impact. Below are some complementary strategies we incorporated:

1. SCAMPER:

The acronym (Substitute, Combine, Adapt, Modify, Put to another use, Eliminate, Reverse) served as a catalyst for idea generation within each circle, offering valuable prompts for creative thinking.

2. Six Thinking Hats:

Edward de Bono's approach enabled us to assess the ideas produced in the Expanding Circles by examining them through various lenses, including logic, emotion, caution, optimism, creativity, and control.

3. Analogical Thinking:

We encouraged participants to draw analogies from other industries or natural systems, especially for the outer circles.

4. Reverse Brainstorming:

Sometimes, we started by asking, "How could we make this problem worse?" and then reversing those ideas, which often led to innovative solutions.

5. Mind Mapping:

We used mind maps to further explore and connect ideas generated in the Expanding Circles.

6. Nominal Group Technique:

This strategy guaranteed that every participant enjoyed an equal chance to present their ideas, effectively tackling the prevalent issue of dominant voices during brainstorming sessions.

By incorporating these methodologies, we succeeded in transforming our innovation sessions into even more effective and inclusive experiences.

Fostering a Culture of Continuous Innovation

Introducing the Expanding Circles method marked merely the start of our journey. To genuinely revolutionize our organization, it was essential to cultivate a culture that embraced ongoing innovation. Below are several strategies we implemented:

From Command To Collaboration: A Journey In Modern Leadership

1. Innovation Time:

We established a policy that allowed employees to dedicate 15% of their time to pursue innovative projects of their choice, utilizing the Expanding Circles method to guide their thought processes.

2. Cross-Functional Innovation Teams:

We formed cross-departmental teams, each assigned the responsibility of tackling a particular challenge through the application of the Expanding Circles method.

3. Innovation Metrics:

We established innovative metrics to evaluate our progress in creativity, focusing on "idea implementation rate" and "the effectiveness of executed ideas" instead of merely tallying the total number of ideas produced.

4. Leadership Modeling:

Leaders were expected to use and advocate for the Expanding Circles method, demonstrating its value through their own actions.

5. Training and Development:

We incorporated innovation skills, including the Expanding Circles method, into our training and development programs.

6. Reward and Recognition:

We created an innovation award program that recognized both incremental improvements and breakthrough ideas.

7. Physical Space:

We redesigned our office space to include "innovation hubs" with circular whiteboards for impromptu Expanding Circles sessions.

Failure Tolerance:

We made a concerted effort to destigmatize the notion of failure, understanding that not every innovative idea will come to fruition and that setbacks frequently offer invaluable insights.

By weaving these practices into the fabric of our organizational culture, we successfully shifted from occasional innovation initiatives to establishing a genuine culture of continuous innovation.

The Expanding Circles method, along with the innovation culture it cultivated, emerged as a pivotal differentiator for our organization. This approach enabled us to harmonize immediate enhancements with long-term visionary strategies, ensuring we remained adaptable and forward-looking in a swiftly evolving business landscape.

As we transition into the next chapter, we will delve into how this innovation strategy converged with our developing understanding of productivity and focus within today's modern workplace.

Chapter 6:
The Myth of Multitasking

The Science of Attention and Focus

As our organization progressed in its methods of leadership and innovation, I started to recognize a widespread misconception that was undermining our productivity and creativity: the notion that multitasking was a beneficial skill that enhanced efficiency. This belief was deeply embedded not only in our company culture but also in the broader societal context. However, as I explored the intricacies of attention and focus, I uncovered a vastly different truth.

The human brain, despite its extraordinary abilities, is fundamentally ill-equipped for multitasking. What we commonly refer to as "multitasking" is, in reality, rapid task-switching, which incurs a considerable cognitive toll.

Key findings from neuroscience and cognitive psychology include:

1. Attention Residue: When we transition from one task to another, our focus doesn't instantaneously shift. A portion of our attention lingers on the prior task, a phenomenon known as "attention residue." This leftover focus diminishes our mental capacity for the new task.

2. Increased Error Rates: Studies have shown that multitasking increases error rates by up to 50%.

3. Cognitive Load: Task-switching imposes a heavy cognitive load, depleting mental resources more quickly than focused work.

4. Reduced Creativity: The constant interruption of task-switching inhibits the deep thinking necessary for creative problem-solving.

5. Stress and Burnout: The mental effort required for frequent task-switching can lead to increased stress and eventual burnout.

One particularly eye-opening study was carried out by Gloria Mark at the University of California. She discovered that the average time it takes to refocus on a task after an interruption is 23 minutes and 15 seconds. In a workplace filled with frequent interruptions, this can result in an astonishing loss of productivity.

Additionally, studies indicate that individuals who frequently multitask tend to perform worse than those who do it infrequently. They are more easily distracted by irrelevant stimuli in their surroundings and struggle to compartmentalize tasks in their minds.

Grasping the science behind attention and focus marked the initial phase of challenging the multitasking myth within our organization. This understanding laid a robust groundwork for the necessary transformations in our work culture and practices.

The True Cost of Task-Switching

Equipped with a solid grasp of the science behind attention and focus, I set out to evaluate the genuine costs associated with task-switching within our organization. The outcomes were nothing short of revealing.

Over the course of a month, we implemented a company-wide study where employees meticulously documented their tasks and interruptions. The insights we uncovered were astonishing:

1. Time Lost: On average, employees were losing 2.1 hours per day to task-switching and recovery time. This amounted to over 10 hours per week per employee.

2. Reduced Quality: Projects characterized by constant task-switching exhibited a staggering 32% increase in error rates and required more revisions compared to those that allowed employees to concentrate for extended periods.

3. Extended Completion Times: Tasks that were frequently interrupted took, on average, 50% longer to complete than similar tasks performed with focus.

4. Stress and Satisfaction: Employees reported higher stress levels and lower job satisfaction on days with frequent task-switching.

5. Creative Output: Teams that dedicated themselves to focused work generated 41% more innovative ideas, according to our innovation metrics, in contrast to teams that frequently engaged in multitasking.

We also looked at the financial implications:

1. Lost Productivity: Based on average salaries, the time lost to task-switching was costing us approximately $1.2 million per year for every 100 employees.

2. Opportunity Cost: Delayed project completions were causing us to miss market opportunities, with an estimated cost of $5 million in the previous year.

3. Employee Turnover: Exit interviews uncovered that the stress stemming from "constantly being busy yet accomplishing little" was a major contributor to employee turnover, leading to significant recruitment and training expenses.

One particularly revealing instance involved our product development team, who had been grappling with missed deadlines and a noticeable decline in output quality. Upon examining their work habits, we discovered they spent an average of 3.5 hours in meetings each day, incessantly checking emails and attempting to manage multiple projects at once.

Consequently, they found it challenging to carve out more than 30 minutes of uninterrupted time for any single task. It was no surprise that their productivity and creativity were significantly compromised.

This assessment highlighted that the costs associated with multitasking were much greater than we had previously understood. It affected not only our productivity but also our creativity, employee satisfaction, and overall financial performance. It became clear that we had to implement substantial changes in how we approached work and managed our time and focus.

Strategies for Effective Single-Tasking

Understanding the substantial toll of multitasking, we embarked on a mission to create and apply strategies that promote effective single-tasking. Below are some of the essential methods we adopted:

1. Time Blocking:

We prompted employees to set aside dedicated time blocks for concentrated work on particular tasks. During these intervals, they were urged to disable notifications and steer clear of distractions.

2. The Pomodoro Technique:

We implemented this time management approach, characterized by working in concentrated 25-minute segments interspersed with brief breaks. Numerous employees discovered that this technique assisted them in sustaining focus and effectively regulating their energy levels throughout the day.

3. Meeting Reforms:

We implemented several changes to our meeting culture:

- Reduced meeting times from 60 to 45 minutes by default

- Required clear agendas for all meetings

- Introduced "No Meeting Wednesdays" to ensure at least one day a week of uninterrupted work time

4. Email Management:

We advocated for batch processing of emails during designated times instead of incessantly checking them. Additionally, we championed the adoption of asynchronous communication tools for handling non-urgent matters.

5. Distraction-Free Zones:

We created quiet spaces in the office where employees could work without interruptions when they needed deep focus.

6. Focus-Friendly Technology:

We provided tools like website blockers and focused apps to help
employees manage digital distractions.

7. Prioritization Techniques:

We trained employees in methods like the Eisenhower Matrix to help
them prioritize tasks and focus on what's truly important.

8. Mindfulness Practices:

We provided mindfulness and meditation training sessions aimed at
enhancing employees' capacity to concentrate and handle distractions
effectively.

A notably effective initiative was our "Focus Fridays." Each Friday
afternoon was set aside as a designated time free from meetings,
allowing for uninterrupted individual work. Employees were
motivated to engage in their most demanding or innovative tasks
during this period.

The outcomes of these strategies were remarkable. In just three
months, we observed a 28% increase in self-reported productivity, a
35% reduction in reported stress levels, and a 40% boost in employee
satisfaction regarding their workload management.

Time Management and Prioritization Techniques

Although establishing an environment conducive to focused work was
essential, we also had to make certain that employees were utilizing
their time efficiently. To address this, we implemented various time
management and prioritization strategies:

1. The Eisenhower Matrix:

We trained employees to categorize tasks based on their urgency and
importance, helping them focus on what truly matters.

2. The 80/20 Rule (Pareto Principle):

We encouraged identifying the 20% of efforts that yield 80% of results, focusing energy on high-impact activities.

3. MIT (Most Important Tasks):

Employees were asked to identify and tackle their 1-3 most important tasks each day before moving on to less critical work.

4. Time Tracking:

We implemented voluntary time tracking, not for surveillance, but to help employees understand how they were actually spending their time.

5. The Two-Minute Rule:

For small tasks that take less than two minutes, we encouraged immediate action rather than scheduling for later, reducing mental clutter.

6. Structured Procrastination:

We introduced the concept of using the urge to procrastinate productively by working on important tasks to avoid other important tasks.

7. Energy Management:

We trained employees to identify their peak energy times and schedule their most important or challenging work accordingly.

8. The Ivy Lee Method:

At the end of each day, employees were encouraged to write down the six most important tasks for the next day, prioritized in order of importance.

One of our team leaders, Sarah, recounted a particularly transformative experience with these techniques. She had been grappling with a persistent sense of being overwhelmed and constantly lagging behind in her tasks. After adopting the Eisenhower Matrix and the Most Important Task (MIT) approach, she observed a remarkable shift. "For the first time in years," she expressed, "I feel in control of my workday instead of being at its mercy."

These time management and prioritization methods, paired with our single-tasking strategies, started to revolutionize the way work was executed within our organization.

Technology: Friend or Foe of Focus?

In our pursuit of enhancing focus and minimizing multitasking, we needed to tackle the intricate influence of technology. Although technology frequently served as a source of distraction, we also acknowledged its capability to boost focus and productivity when utilized with intention.

We adopted a nuanced approach to technology:

1. Audit of Digital Tools:

We carried out a comprehensive evaluation of the digital tools utilized across the company, removing unnecessary or distracting applications and consolidating around the most efficient options.

2. Notification Management:

We offered training sessions focused on effectively managing notifications across various devices, motivating employees to disable non-essential alerts during dedicated work periods.

3. Email Alternatives:

To enhance internal communication, we transitioned to asynchronous communication tools that allowed for flexibility and did not require immediate responses while reserving email for external interactions and formal communications.

4. Focus-Enhancing Apps:

We compiled a carefully selected list of suggested applications for tracking time, blocking distracting websites, and boosting focus, empowering employees to select the tools that suited their individual needs best.

5. Digital Detox Periods:

We encouraged periodic "digital detox" times, especially during creative tasks or strategic planning sessions.

6. Mindful Technology Use:

We offered comprehensive training focused on the mindful use of technology, enabling employees to gain greater awareness of their digital behaviors and make intentional decisions regarding their tech interactions.

7. Tech-Free Meetings:

For specific meeting types, particularly those focused on brainstorming or strategy, we tried out tech-free formats to promote deeper engagement and minimize distractions.

8. AI and Automation:

We investigated how AI and automation could take over repetitive tasks, enabling human focus for more intricate and creative projects.

A particularly compelling case study surfaced from our marketing team. They had faced persistent disruptions from numerous digital marketing tools. By streamlining their tools, batching social media efforts, and implementing scheduling software, they successfully cut down the time spent on routine tasks by 40%, creating more room for strategic planning and creative endeavors.

Although we didn't find a flawless solution, this well-rounded strategy toward technology allowed us to leverage its advantages while minimizing its capacity for distraction.

Case Studies in Implementing Focus-Friendly Policies

Establishing focus-enhancing policies throughout the organization proved to be a major initiative. Below are several case studies that highlight our methodology and outcomes:

Case Study 1: Product Development Team

Challenge: The team was struggling with constant interruptions and fragmented work time, leading to missed deadlines and quality issues.

Solution:

- Implemented "Core Focus Hours" from 10am to 2pm daily, during which meetings were prohibited, and response to non-urgent communication was not expected.

- Introduced "No Meeting Wednesdays" for uninterrupted work on complex problems.

- Trained the team in the Pomodoro Technique and provided noise-cancelling headphones.

Results:

- Project completion times reduced by 25%

- Quality issues decreased by 30%

- Team reported a 40% increase in job satisfaction

Case Study 2: Customer Service Department

Challenge: Representatives were juggling multiple channels (phone, email, chat) simultaneously, leading to increased errors and customer dissatisfaction.

Solution:

- Restructured workflows so representatives focused on one channel at a time in 2-hour blocks.

- Implemented a new ticketing system that allowed for better task prioritization.

- Provided training on mindfulness techniques to improve focus during customer interactions.

Results:

- Customer satisfaction scores improved by 22%

- Average handle time decreased by 15%

- Employee turnover in the department reduced by 30%

Case Study 3: Executive Leadership Team

Challenge: Leadership was setting a poor example with constant multitasking during meetings and expecting immediate responses to emails at all hours.

Solution:

- Instituted a "devices off" policy for most meetings.

- Established "email curfew" hours (no sending emails between 8pm and 7am).

- Each leader committed to two hours of focused, uninterrupted work daily.

Results:

- Meeting times were reduced by 35% due to increased efficiency

- Improved work-life balance reported by 80% of the leadership team

- This change cascaded through the organization, shifting the overall culture

These case studies revealed that although the unique execution of focus-enhancing policies had to be customized to meet the specific requirements of each team, the overarching principles could effectively be implemented across various sectors of the organization.

Measuring Productivity: Quality over Quantity

As we transitioned to a culture prioritizing focused work, we recognized that our conventional metrics for assessing productivity were insufficient. Merely counting hours worked or tasks accomplished failed to reflect the true worth of deep, concentrated effort. It became essential to create new metrics that highlighted quality instead of quantity.

Here's how we approached this challenge:

1. Outcome-Based Metrics:

Rather than focusing on measuring activities, we redirected our efforts to assess outcomes. For instance, within our software development team, we transitioned from tallying lines of code to evaluating how new features influence user engagement.

2. Quality Metrics:

We put greater emphasis on quality metrics such as error rates, customer satisfaction scores, and the number of revisions required for projects.

3. Innovation Metrics:

We developed ways to measure innovative output, such as the number of new ideas implemented and their impact on the business.

4. Focus Time Tracking:

Although we aimed to avoid being overly prescriptive, we actively promoted the voluntary tracking of focus time, acknowledging and celebrating enhancements in our capacity to sustain prolonged concentration.

5. Employee Satisfaction:

We acknowledged that employees who feel satisfied are frequently more productive. Therefore, we integrated metrics for job satisfaction and work-life balance into our assessments of productivity.

6. Collaboration Quality:

We developed metrics to assess the quality of collaboration, recognizing that effective teamwork often leads to higher productivity.

7. Learning and Growth:

We included metrics related to skill development and knowledge sharing, acknowledging that learning contributes to long-term productivity.

8. Value Creation:

For positions where output was difficult to quantify, we collaborated with employees to establish a clear definition of what value creation entailed in their specific roles and how it could be effectively measured.

A particularly impactful modification occurred in our evaluation process for the sales team. In the past, we concentrated predominantly on activity metrics, such as the number of calls made or emails sent. We transitioned to a model that emphasized the quality of customer relationships cultivated, the strategic alignment of closed deals, and the long-term potential of secured accounts.

This refreshed approach to productivity measurement not only reinforced our commitment to quality work but also motivated employees to focus on significant tasks over mere busy work, encouraging them to discover avenues for creating genuine value rather than simply looking occupied.

The transition came with its own set of challenges. Some managers initially found it difficult to adapt, feeling a loss of control when they could no longer monitor every minute of their team's time. However, as positive results emerged in terms of enhanced output and higher employee satisfaction, even the most doubtful were ultimately persuaded.

By redefining our productivity metrics, we aligned them with our goals of promoting deep work and nurturing a focus-friendly environment.

From Command To Collaboration: A Journey In Modern Leadership

This alignment not only boosted our actual productivity but also solidified the cultural shifts we aimed to achieve.

As we reach the end of this chapter, it's evident that dispelling the myth of multitasking and cultivating a culture of concentrated work has been a transformative journey for our organization. This evolution necessitated changes in our work structure, technology usage, and even our success measurement criteria. The outcomes, however, were undeniably positive: increased productivity, enhanced work quality, greater employee satisfaction, and ultimately, improved business results.

In the upcoming chapter, we will delve into how these modifications in our work approach intertwined with our growing understanding of emotional intelligence in leadership.

Chapter 7:
Emotional Intelligence in Leadership

Understanding Emotional Intelligence

As our organization transformed its approach to leadership, innovation, and productivity, I started to identify a vital element that served as the foundation for all these aspects: emotional intelligence (EI). My military training had prioritized technical expertise and decisiveness, but I was beginning to realize that in today's intricate, human-focused business landscape, EI was equally essential, if not more so.

Emotional intelligence, according to psychologists Peter Salovey and John Mayer, refers to "the ability to monitor one's own and others' feelings and emotions, to differentiate among them, and to utilize this information to inform one's thoughts and actions." The concept was later popularized by Daniel Goleman, who delineated it into five fundamental components:

1. Self-awareness: The ability to recognize and understand your own emotions.

2. Self-regulation: The ability to control and manage your emotions.

3. Motivation: The ability to motivate yourself and others.

4. Empathy: The ability to recognize and understand others' emotions.

5. Social skills: The ability to manage relationships and navigate social networks.

As I explored the concept of emotional intelligence (EI) more thoroughly, I recognized its essential role in effective leadership. Leaders who possess a high level of EI demonstrate a greater capacity to:

From Command To Collaboration: A Journey In Modern Leadership

- Understand and manage their own emotions, leading to more balanced decision-making

- Empathize with their team members, fostering trust and loyalty

- Motivate and inspire others, even in challenging circumstances

- Navigate complex social dynamics and build strong relationships

- Handle conflict more effectively

- Adapt to change and help others do the same

One study that truly resonated with me was conducted by TalentSmart, revealing that emotional intelligence stands out as the most significant predictor of performance, accounting for an impressive 58% of success across various job types. Moreover, a striking 90% of top performers demonstrated high emotional intelligence.

These insights mirrored my personal experiences. I found myself reflecting on moments where my deficit in EI had sparked misunderstandings or conflicts, alongside times when a more emotionally attuned approach led to significant breakthroughs.

For instance, during my early transition into civilian leadership, I worked with a talented team member named Alex, who repeatedly failed to meet deadlines. Initially, my emotionally unintelligent reaction was to reprimand him severely, which only resulted in Alex becoming defensive and detached.

Eventually, armed with a deeper understanding of EI, I chose to handle the situation differently. I made it a priority to engage in a one-on-one conversation with Alex, posing open-ended questions and genuinely listening to his feedback. I uncovered that he was grappling with a family illness that was impacting his work. By expressing empathy and collaborating with Alex to modify his workload while offering support, we were able to enhance both his performance and his dedication to the team.

This encounter, along with many similar instances, solidified my belief in the importance of cultivating emotional intelligence—not just within myself but across our organization. It became evident that EI transcended mere "soft" skills; it was a crucial element of effective leadership and a vital driver of organizational success.

The Five Components of EI in Leadership

In order to seamlessly weave emotional intelligence into our leadership practices, we recognized the necessity of understanding and enhancing each of its five core components. Below is an outline of our approach to each element:

1. Self-awareness:

We initiated consistent self-reflection exercises for our leaders, incorporating practices like journaling and mindfulness. Additionally, we established 360-degree feedback systems to provide leaders with insights into how they were perceived by others.

For instance, our CFO, who had typically been regarded as brusque and unapproachable, was taken aback when feedback revealed that her communication style was inducing anxiety among her team. This newfound awareness prompted her to intentionally soften her approach, leading to enhanced team dynamics and improved performance.

2. Self-regulation:

We implemented comprehensive training programs focused on stress management techniques and urged leaders to exemplify suitable emotional responses, particularly during high-pressure scenarios.

For instance, in the midst of a crisis where a significant project was on the brink of failure, I made a deliberate effort to control my stress and anxiety. By maintaining a composed and focused demeanor, I was able to assist the team in thinking clearly and formulating a solution rather than giving in to panic.

3. Motivation:

We focused on guiding leaders to intertwine their personal values with the overarching mission of the organization. Additionally, we equipped them with strategies to inspire and intrinsically motivate their teams, moving beyond mere extrinsic rewards.

For example, our Head of Product Development facilitated a session in which team members openly shared their personal motivations for working in the tech industry. By connecting project objectives to these individual motivations, she significantly enhanced team engagement and creativity.

4. Empathy:

We introduced "empathy walks," allowing leaders to immerse themselves in various roles within the organization, fostering a deeper understanding of diverse perspectives. Additionally, we offered training sessions focused on enhancing active listening skills.

For instance, after spending a day in customer service, our COO acquired fresh insights into the hurdles encountered by our front-line employees. This experience prompted several policy adjustments that significantly boosted both employee satisfaction and customer experience.

5. Social skills:

We concentrated on enhancing leaders' skills in conflict resolution, negotiation, and team building. Additionally, we promoted cross-departmental networking to dismantle silos within the organization.

For example, our Head of Sales, recognized for his outstanding individual contributions, made a concerted effort to refine his team-building capabilities. By prioritizing the development of his team members over merely focusing on his own sales achievements, he successfully boosted overall department performance by 30%.

By emphasizing these five key components, we experienced marked improvements in leadership effectiveness throughout the organization. Leaders grew more self-aware, adept at managing their own emotions as well as those of their teams, and increasingly inspiring. They also became more empathetic toward diverse perspectives and more proficient in navigating intricate social dynamics.

The outcome was a leadership culture infused with emotional intelligence, enabling us to tackle the challenges posed by our fast-evolving business landscape more effectively.

Developing Emotional Intelligence

Identifying the importance of emotional intelligence was just the first step. The real challenge lies in developing these skills throughout our organization. We implemented a multi-faceted approach to cultivating EI:

1. Assessment:

We initiated a comprehensive, organization-wide emotional intelligence (EI) assessment to create a foundational baseline and pinpoint specific areas for enhancement. To achieve this, we utilized instruments such as the Emotional and Social Competency Inventory (ESCI) and the Mayer-Salovey-Caruso Emotional Intelligence Test (MSCEIT).

2. Training Programs:

We designed a comprehensive series of workshops that concentrated on each facet of emotional intelligence (EI). These sessions were far from purely theoretical; they incorporated hands-on exercises and role-playing activities, allowing participants to practice EI skills in practical, real-world contexts.

3. Coaching:

We implemented individualized coaching sessions for leaders, focusing on their unique emotional intelligence (EI) growth requirements. This tailored method fostered specific enhancements and ensured a sense of accountability.

4. Peer Learning Groups:

We established small groups where leaders could discuss EI challenges, share experiences, and learn from each other in a safe, supportive environment.

5. Experiential Learning:

We created opportunities for leaders to practice EI skills in low-stakes situations before applying them to more critical scenarios.

6. Integration into Performance Reviews:

We incorporated EI competencies into our performance evaluation process, signaling their importance to career development within the organization.

7. Modeling from the Top:

As the leadership team, we dedicated ourselves to actively pursuing our own emotional intelligence (EI) growth, transparently sharing our challenges and achievements to foster a culture of ongoing emotional development.

8. Mindfulness and Reflection:

We implemented mindfulness practices and promoted ongoing self-reflection to improve self-awareness and emotional regulation.

One particularly impactful initiative was our "EI Challenge of the Month." Each month, we concentrated on a particular EI skill, providing daily tips, weekly challenges, and a reflective session at the end of the month. For instance, during "Empathy Month," leaders were tasked with engaging in at least one empathetic conversation daily, maintaining a journal of their experiences and insights.

Additionally, we discovered that storytelling served as a potent method for cultivating EI. We urged leaders to recount experiences in which they effectively (or ineffectively) utilized EI skills, thereby making the concepts more relatable and applicable in real-life scenarios.

The journey toward developing EI was not a rapid endeavor. It demanded consistent dedication and an openness to vulnerability while recognizing areas for growth. However, over time, we witnessed substantial shifts in how our leaders tackled challenges, interacted with their teams, and made decisions.

Empathy as a Leadership Tool

Among all the facets of emotional intelligence, we discovered that empathy significantly influenced leadership effectiveness. Empathy—the capacity to comprehend and resonate with the emotions of others—emerged as a formidable asset for fostering trust, enhancing communication, and boosting team performance.

We focused on developing three types of empathy in our leaders:

1. Cognitive Empathy: The ability to understand how someone else might be thinking or feeling.

2. Emotional Empathy: The ability to share the feelings of another person.

3. Compassionate Empathy: The ability to understand someone's feelings and take action to help.

Here are some of the ways we cultivated empathy in our leadership:

1. Active Listening Training:

We implemented training focused on active listening skills, highlighting the necessity of fully engaging with the speaker, refraining from interruptions, and delivering considerate responses.

2. Perspective-Taking Exercises:

We introduced exercises where leaders had to articulate situations from the perspective of different stakeholders, helping them consider multiple viewpoints.

3. Cross-Departmental Shadowing:

Leaders spend time in different parts of the organization to gain a firsthand understanding of various roles and challenges.

4. Customer Empathy Mapping:

We used empathy mapping techniques not just for understanding customers but also for team members and other stakeholders.

5. Emotion Recognition Training:

We provided training in recognizing facial expressions and body language to improve leaders' ability to pick up on emotional cues.

6. Personal Story Sharing:

We fostered an environment that encouraged the sharing of personal narratives in team settings, aiming to strengthen emotional bonds and enhance mutual understanding.

A striking illustration of empathy's impact emerged from our IT department. This department had long struggled with a reputation for being unresponsive and challenging to collaborate with. The newly appointed IT Director, Mark, committed himself to transforming this perception through the power of empathy.

Paul launched an initiative where IT team members would dedicate one day each month to work alongside their internal "customers" in other departments. This initiative provided them with firsthand insights into the difficulties and frustrations encountered by non-IT staff when navigating technology-related issues.

The outcomes were nothing short of revolutionary. IT personnel began addressing support requests with heightened understanding and patience. They took the initiative to reach out to other departments, preemptively addressing potential issues before they escalated. Communication improved significantly, resulting in a 70% increase in satisfaction with IT services within just six months.

This case illustrated the effectiveness of empathy not merely as a personal skill but as a strategic leadership asset capable of facilitating substantial organizational advancements.

Case Studies in Emotionally Intelligent Leadership

To show the real-world impact of emotionally intelligent leadership, let's examine a few case studies from our organization:

Case Study 1: The Struggling Team

Situation: Our marketing team was underperforming, with missed deadlines and internal conflicts.

EI Approach: The new team leader, Sarah, used her emotional intelligence skills to transform the team:

- She held one-on-one meetings with each team member, practicing active listening to understand their perspectives and challenges.

- She used her self-awareness to recognize and manage her own frustration with the team's performance.

- She demonstrated empathy by acknowledging the stress the team was under and worked collaboratively to find solutions.

- She used her social skills to mediate conflicts and build stronger relationships within the team.

Result: Within three months, team productivity increased by 40%, and employee satisfaction scores rose from 65% to 89%.

Case Study 2: The Difficult Client

Situation: A major client was threatening to leave due to dissatisfaction with our services.

EI Approach: The account manager, Tom, applied EI principles to salvage the relationship:

- He used self-regulation to manage his defensive reactions to the client's criticism.

- He practiced empathy to truly understand the client's frustrations and needs.

- He motivated his team to see this as an opportunity for improvement rather than a failure.

- He used his social skills to rebuild trust with the client and negotiate a path forward.

Result: Not only was the client relationship saved, but it became one of our strongest partnerships, with the client increasing their business with us by 30% the following year.

Case Study 3: The Change Initiative

Situation: We needed to implement a significant organizational change that was causing anxiety and resistance among employees.

EI Approach: The change management team, led by Alicia, used EI to guide the process:

- They demonstrated self-awareness by acknowledging their own uncertainties about the change.

- They used empathy to understand and address employee concerns.

- They leveraged their motivational skills to inspire enthusiasm for the new direction.

- They employed social skills to build a coalition of change advocates across the organization.

Result: The transition was executed seamlessly, as 85% of employees indicated they felt acknowledged and supported during the entire process. The initiative was finalized on schedule and successfully met its intended objectives.

These case studies illustrate how emotional intelligence can be effectively leveraged to tackle a range of leadership challenges, encompassing team dynamics, client interactions, and organizational transformations. In every scenario, EI skills played a pivotal role in securing positive results.

By cultivating and utilizing emotional intelligence, our leaders succeeded in fostering more engaged teams, establishing stronger connections, and adeptly handling complex challenges. This emotionally attuned approach to leadership emerged as a vital element of our organization's achievements, propelling advancements in performance, innovation, and employee satisfaction.

As we wrap up this chapter, it is evident that emotional intelligence is far more than a desirable soft skill; it is an essential component of effective leadership in today's business landscape. By nurturing EI within our leaders and across the organization, we succeeded in cultivating a more resilient, adaptive, and high-performing culture.

In the upcoming chapter, we will delve into how this emotionally intelligent leadership style aligns with the challenges of building and guiding high-performance teams.

Chapter 8:
Building and Leading High-Performance Teams

Characteristics of High-Performance Team

As our organization progressed in its approach to leadership, innovation, and emotional intelligence, we shifted our attention to the essential task of developing and guiding high-performance teams. Through both practical experience and in-depth research, we uncovered several crucial traits that distinguish high-performance teams from the rest:

Clear, Compelling Purpose:

High-performance teams possess a unified sense of purpose, one that resonates with the organization's broader objectives and aligns with the personal values of each member. This collective purpose serves as a guiding star, shaping decision-making and driving the motivation of the entire team.

Strong Leadership:

These high-performing teams are guided by leaders who not only practice emotional intelligence but also deliver clear, decisive direction. They cultivate a culture of trust and ensure a space where psychological safety thrives.

Defined Roles and Responsibilities:

Each team member fully grasps their specific role and recognizes how it ties into the broader mission. There's a clear understanding of duties, yet enough flexibility to adapt as needed.

Open and Transparent Communication:

High-performance teams engage in open, direct, and regular communication. They embrace tough conversations and aren't hesitant to offer constructive criticism when needed.

Trust and Psychological Safety:

Team members are encouraged to embrace risks, voice their ideas, and learn from their mistakes without the threat of punishment. This sense of psychological safety promotes creativity and growth.

Diversity and Inclusion:

These teams leverage diverse perspectives, experiences, and skills. They actively work to ensure all voices are heard and valued.

Continuous Learning and Improvement:

High-performance teams have a growth mindset. They regularly reflect on their processes and outcomes, always looking for ways to improve.

Results-Oriented:

While they value process and relationships, high-performance teams are ultimately focused on achieving results and meeting or exceeding their goals.

Adaptability:

These teams are able to pivot quickly in response to changes in their environment or new challenges.

Mutual Accountability:

Team members take responsibility for their own actions and hold each other accountable for the team's overall success.

We found that these traits were mutually reinforcing. For example, fostering psychological safety encouraged open dialogue, which subsequently strengthened trust and enabled more effective collective accountability.

One team that exemplified these traits was our product development team. Under the leadership of Anna, who possesses exceptional emotional intelligence, the team was driven by a clear mission: to develop products that genuinely enhanced our customers' lives. While their roles were clearly outlined, they also enjoyed the freedom to engage in various areas of expertise. Their stand-up meetings were perfect examples of transparent communication, where team members openly discussed challenges and collaborated on solutions.

The team's diversity—encompassing various professional backgrounds, thinking styles, and personal experiences—sparked innovative ideas. They maintained a rigorous process for learning from both their successes and setbacks, which allowed them to refine their strategies continuously. Most importantly, they consistently produced high-quality products that were delivered on schedule and within budget.

By understanding and nurturing these attributes, we initiated the transformation of all our teams into high-performance units.

Strategies for Team Formation and Development

Building high-performance teams doesn't happen by chance. We developed several strategies for intentionally forming and developing teams:

Purposeful Team Composition:

We progressed past the mere act of gathering individuals equipped with the right technical skills. We took into account various elements such as cognitive styles, personality traits, and individual work preferences to forge well-rounded teams. We employed assessments like the Myers-Briggs Type Indicator and the Belbin Team Role Inventory to guide our choices.

Clear Charter and Goals:

Each team initiated their journey with a well-defined charter that detailed their objectives, areas of responsibility, and crucial performance metrics. This charter was crafted collectively to guarantee commitment and ownership from all team members.

Team Kick-off Workshops:

New teams began with intensive workshops aimed at harmonizing objectives, setting behavioral standards, and initiating relationship-building. These workshops included team-building exercises and candid dialogues regarding individual working style and expectations.

Defined Decision-Making Processes:

We established well-defined procedures for how decisions would be made within the team, utilizing approaches such as consensus, consultation, or alternative strategies tailored to the situation.

Regular Team Health Checks:

We instituted quarterly team health checks, using tools like the Team Effectiveness Survey to identify areas for improvement.

Cross-functional Exposure:

We produced opportunities for team members to work on projects outside their core team, promoting broader organizational understanding and networks.

Skill Development Plans:

Each team had a skill development plan that identified key competencies needed for success and strategies for developing these skills.

Celebration and Recognition:

We made a point of regularly celebrating team successes and recognizing both individual and collective achievements.

Conflict Resolution Training:

Recognizing that conflict is inevitable in high-performance teams, we provided training in constructive conflict resolution techniques.

Leadership Development:

We dedicated resources to cultivate leadership capabilities across all levels of the team, extending beyond just the designated team leader.

One particularly successful initiative was our "Team Incubator" program. Newly formed teams spent their initial month in a specialized environment, shielded from day-to-day operational demands. This period was devoted to team-building exercises, enhancing skills, and planning their approach to their mission.

For instance, when we assembled a new cross-functional team to spearhead our digital transformation project, they utilized their first month in the Team Incubator. They emerged with a unified vision, clearly defined roles and processes, and robust interpersonal connections. This commitment to team development yielded significant results, enabling them to successfully navigate one of the most pivotal changes in our organization's history.

These strategies empowered us to consistently assemble teams that could rapidly achieve high-performance levels and maintain them over time.

Fostering Trust and Psychological Safety

We uncovered that trust and psychological safety serve as essential pillars for developing high-performance teams. Psychological safety, a concept articulated by Harvard Business School professor Amy Edmondson, is defined as "a shared belief held by members of a team that the team is safe for interpersonal risk-taking."

Here are some of the strategies we employed to foster trust and psychological safety:

Lead by Example:

Leaders modeled vulnerability by admitting mistakes, asking for help, and encouraging feedback. This sent a powerful message that it was safe for others to do the same.

Encourage and Reward Risk-Taking:

We celebrated intelligent risk-taking, even when it didn't lead to success. This encouraged innovation and learning.

Practice Active Listening:

We trained all team members in active listening techniques, emphasizing the importance of seeking to understand before being understood.

Implement a "No Blame" Culture:

We shifted from a "who's at fault" mentality to a "what can we learn" approach when things went wrong.

Create Opportunities for Social Bonding:

We organized both formal and informal activities to help team members build personal connections.

Use Inclusive Meeting Practices:

We implemented techniques like round-robin participation and anonymous idea submission to ensure all voices were heard.

Provide Feedback Training:

We trained team members in how to give and receive constructive feedback effectively.

Establish Team Agreements:

Each team collaboratively developed a set of agreements about how they would work together and treat each other.

Regular Check-ins:

We encouraged recurrent one-on-one check-ins between team leaders and members, focusing not just on tasks but on well-being and job satisfaction.

Address Microaggressions Promptly:

We provided training focused on identifying and confronting microaggressions, ensuring that every team member felt respected and valued.

One particularly noteworthy example of psychological safety in action was our customer experience team. The team leader, Michael, consistently opened each meeting by sharing a mistake he had made or a valuable lesson he had learned. This level of transparency fostered a culture where team members felt encouraged to share their own experiences.

In one memorable instance, a team member named Lisa put forth a bold proposal to completely overhaul our customer onboarding process. In numerous organizations, such a daring suggestion might be disregarded or met with criticism. However, within this psychologically safe environment, the team engaged in a constructive discussion regarding the idea. Although the exact proposal wasn't adopted, various elements of it contributed to substantial enhancements in our onboarding process.

The outcome of nurturing this psychologically safe atmosphere was a team that regularly generated innovative ideas, swiftly identified and resolved challenges, and achieved impressive levels of both performance and job satisfaction.

By placing a strong emphasis on trust and psychological safety, we cultivated environments where team members felt empowered to bring their authentic selves to work, take calculated risks, and collaborate effectively.

Managing Conflict and Diversity

As we built more varied teams and encouraged open communication, we recognized the need to effectively manage conflict and influence diversity for better outcomes. We came to see positive conflict as a sign of a healthy, high-performing team rather than something to be avoided.

Here are some strategies we implemented:

Diversity and Inclusion Training:

We provided comprehensive training on unconscious bias, cultural competence, and the value of diverse perspectives.

Conflict Resolution Framework:

We introduced a step-by-step framework for addressing conflicts, emphasizing finding win-win solutions.

Cognitive Diversity Mapping:

Teams mapped out their cognitive diversity - different thinking styles, problem-solving approaches, and perspectives. This helped them appreciate and leverage their differences.

Structured Debate:

We introduced techniques like "devil's advocate" and "pre-mortems" to encourage healthy debate and diverse viewpoints.

Cultural Intelligence Development:

For our global teams, we invested in developing cultural intelligence to improve cross-cultural collaboration.

Inclusive Language Guidelines:

We developed and implemented guidelines for using inclusive language in all communications.

Conflict Meditation Training:

Select team members were trained as conflict mediators to help resolve disputes when needed.

Regular Diversity Check-ins:

Teams periodically assessed how well they were leveraging their diversity and identified areas for improvement.

Cross-cultural Mentoring:

We established mentoring relationships that crossed cultural, generational, and departmental lines.

Diversity Goals:

We set specific, measurable objectives aimed at enhancing diversity and inclusion across all levels of the organization.

A prime example of effective conflict management and the power of diversity was our global marketing team. This team, distributed across three continents, initially faced challenges with miscommunications and clashing work styles.

The team leader, Priya, adopted a variety of strategies to tackle these issues. She guided the team in creating a cognitive diversity map, which unveiled a rich array of perspectives and problem-solving approaches. This map became a valuable tool for her in task assignments and structuring discussions.

Priya also rolled out a conflict resolution framework designed to empower the team to confront issues candidly and constructively. For instance, during a particularly intense disagreement over the direction of a major campaign, instead of smoothing over the conflict, Priya seized the moment to help the team practice their conflict resolution techniques.

Utilizing their framework, the team was able to articulate differing viewpoints, discover common ground, and ultimately craft an innovative campaign that integrated ideas from various perspectives. This not only resolved the immediate conflict but also fostered a more robust and creative outcome.

Over time, the team began to view their diversity as a significant asset rather than a point of contention. They became recognized for their innovative, globally resonant campaigns that drew inspiration from their diverse perspectives.

By skillfully managing conflict and embracing diversity, we transformed potential divisions into powerful catalysts for creativity and enhanced performance.

Case Studies of Exceptional Teams Across Industries

To illustrate the principles of high-performance teams in action, let's examine a few case studies from different industries:

Case Study 1: Tech Startup Product Team

A small product team at a tech startup was assigned the challenge of creating a new app amidst fierce competition in the marketplace. This team exhibited several high-performance characteristics:

- **Clear Purpose:** The team had a compelling vision of creating an app that would significantly improve users' daily lives.

- **Psychological Safety:** The team leader fostered an environment where members felt safe to propose radical ideas and admit mistakes.

- **Diversity:** The team included members with diverse backgrounds in technology, design, and user experience.

- **Adaptability:** They used agile methodologies to quickly pivot based on user feedback.

Result: The team developed an award-winning app in record time, which quickly gained a large user base and positioned the startup as an industry leader.

Case Study 2: Hospital Emergency Department

An emergency department at a large urban hospital transformed itself into a high-performance team:

- **Defined Roles:** They implemented a clear system of roles and responsibilities that could flex based on the situation.

- **Communication:** They developed a concise, standardized communication protocol to ensure critical information was never lost.

- Continuous Learning: The team held regular debriefs after major incidents to identify lessons learned.

- Trust: Through team-building exercises and shared experiences, they developed a high level of trust that was crucial in high-pressure situations.

Result: The department significantly reduced wait times, improved patient outcomes, and became a model for other hospitals nationwide.

Case Study 3: Manufacturing Plant Safety Team

A safety team at a manufacturing plant exemplified high performance:

- Compelling Purpose: The team rallied around the goal of achieving zero workplace accidents.

- Open Communication: They implemented an anonymous reporting system for safety concerns, ensuring all issues were brought to light.

- Results-Oriented: The team set clear, measurable safety targets and publicly tracked progress.

- Empowerment: Team members were given the authority to stop production if they identified a safety risk.

Result: The plant achieved two years without a lost-time accident, a record in the company's history, and significantly improved overall productivity.

These case studies illustrate that the concepts behind high-performance teams can be effectively implemented in a wide array of industries and environments. Whether within the dynamic atmosphere of a tech startup, the critical nature of a medical facility, or the conventional realm of manufacturing, essential components such as a clear purpose, robust communication, trust, and an emphasis on results contributed to exceptional outcomes.

By studying and implementation of these principles, we consistently nurtured high-performance teams throughout our organization, elevating innovation, productivity, and employee satisfaction to unprecedented levels.

As we wrap up this chapter, it's evident that the process of building and leading high-performance teams is a blend of both art and science. It demands a deliberate commitment to team formation, the cultivation of trust and psychological safety, proficient conflict and diversity management, and an unwavering focus on the key traits that promote high performance. When executed effectively, the outcomes can be revolutionary, benefiting not only the team members but also the organization as a whole.

In our concluding chapter, we will reflect on the comprehensive journey of leadership transformation, transitioning from military command to collaborative civilian leadership, and cast our eyes toward the future of leadership in an ever-evolving business landscape.

Chapter 9:
Reflections and Future Directions

The Journey from Command to Collaboration

As we arrive at the end of this book, it's essential to reflect on the profound transformation we've experienced—shifting from the rigid, hierarchical framework of military leadership to the collaborative and emotionally intelligent strategies demanded in today's civilian organizations.

My journey began in the disciplined atmosphere of the military, where leadership often equated to command. The hierarchy was unmistakably defined, orders were expected to be executed without hesitation, and the mission took precedence above all else. This method had its merits—it cultivated decisiveness, clarity of purpose, and the capacity to respond rapidly in high-stress situations.

However, as I moved into civilian leadership, I quickly discovered that this command-oriented style frequently proved ineffective and occasionally detrimental. The civilian workforce emphasized autonomy, creativity, and personal fulfillment alongside organizational objectives. They wanted leaders who could inspire and empower rather than simply direct and control.

This realization kicked off a profound period of learning and adaptation. I had to unlearn many of the habits that had served me well in the military and develop a new set of skills:

1. From giving orders to asking questions

2. From rigid hierarchy to flexible, collaborative structures

3. From uniformity to embracing and leveraging diversity

4. From suppressing emotions to developing emotional intelligence

5. From focusing solely on the mission to balancing organizational goals with individual needs

The journey wasn't easy. There were moments of frustration, missteps, and the lure to fall back on familiar command-and-control tactics. But with each challenge, I gained new insights and refined my approach.

Key milestones in this journey included:

- Learning the power of asking instead of telling

- Developing a more nuanced understanding of motivation in civilian contexts

- Embracing vulnerability and emotional intelligence as leadership strengths

- Recognizing the value of diverse perspectives in decision-making

- Understanding the importance of creating psychologically safe environments for high performance

This evolution in leadership approach wasn't merely a personal evolution—it mirrored significant shifts in our comprehension of effective leadership within complex, fast-paced environments. As organizations have evolved into flatter structures, embraced greater diversity, and increasingly relied on knowledge-based work, the demand for collaborative and emotionally intelligent leadership has intensified.

Key Lessons Learned

Throughout this journey, several key lessons emerged that fundamentally shaped my approach to leadership:

Emotional Intelligence is Crucial:

Perhaps the most profound insights gained was the crucial role of emotional intelligence in effective leadership. Mastering the ability to comprehend and regulate one's own emotions, along with recognizing and influencing the feelings of others, emerged as an essential competency for inspiring teams, addressing conflicts, and maneuvering through intricate organizational dynamics.

Leadership is About Empowerment:

I discovered that genuine leadership in civilian settings revolves less around possessing all the answers and more around enabling others to discover solutions. By posing the right questions and fostering an atmosphere where individuals felt secure in taking risks, I could unleash significantly greater creativity and innovation than if I simply dictated orders.

Diversity is a Strength to be Leveraged:

Within the military, conformity was frequently valued. However, in the civilian sector, I discovered that diversity—encompassing thought, experience, and background—served as an incredible advantage when effectively harnessed. Cultivating diverse teams and fostering inclusive environments emerged as a crucial strategy for enhancing innovation and boosting performance.

Adaptability is Non-Negotiable:

The rapid evolution of the business landscape highlighted that adaptability is not merely a nice-to-have; it's a fundamental necessity. Leaders must embrace uncertainty and be equipped to adjust their strategies quickly in reaction to shifting conditions.

Culture Eats Strategy for Breakfast:

I learned the truth of Peter Drucker's famous quote. Regardless of how exceptional a strategy is, it stands little chance of success without a supportive organizational culture. Thus, fostering a robust and uplifting culture became a key focus of my leadership efforts.

Trust and Psychological Safety are Foundational:

Creating an environment where team members feel safe to take relational risks - to speak up, share ideas, and admit mistakes - proved to be fundamental to high performance.

Continuous Learning is Essential:

The rapidly growing business landscape made it clear that leadership development is never "finished." Promoting a growth mindset and committing to continuous learning became a core part of my leadership philosophy.

Balance is Key:

While the military experience instilled in me the significance of sacrifice for a mission, my transition to civilian leadership revealed the critical need to balance organizational demands with the well-being of individuals. Achieving sustainable high performance necessitates a focus on work-life balance and prioritizing employee wellness.

Communication Must be Multi-Directional:

Effective leadership communication isn't just about clearly conveying directions - it's about promoting open dialogue, actively listening, and ensuring all voices are heard.

Purpose Drives Performance:

I learned the profound impact of linking individual responsibilities to a broader, meaningful purpose. When individuals grasp how their contributions align with a compelling mission, both motivation and performance see a natural surge.

These insights, hard-earned through personal experience and deep reflection, became the cornerstone of my leadership philosophy. They informed my decision-making, influenced my interactions with team members, and ultimately fostered a more effective and fulfilling leadership style.

The Evolving Landscape of Leadership

As we look to the future, it's clear that the landscape of leadership will continue to evolve. Several trends are shaping the future of leadership:

Digital Transformation:

The ongoing digital revolution is changing how we work, communicate, and make decisions. Leaders of the future will need to be digitally savvy, able to leverage AI and other emerging technologies, and capable of leading remote and hybrid teams effectively.

Globalization:

Despite some recent trends toward localization, the business landscape continues to be profoundly interconnected. Upcoming leaders must possess robust cross-cultural skills and the capacity to effectively manage diverse, global teams.

Sustainability and Social Responsibility:

There's an increasing expectation for businesses to be socially responsible and environmentally sustainable. Leaders will need to balance profit motives with broader societal and environmental concerns.

The Rise of the Gig Economy:

As more workers opt for freelance and contract work, leaders will need to adapt to managing a workforce that's more fluid and less usually structured.

From Command To Collaboration: A Journey In Modern Leadership

Generational Shifts:

With Gen Z entering the workforce and Millennials moving into leadership positions, expectations around work culture, purpose, and leadership styles are shifting.

Rapid Pace of Change:

The pace of technological and social change continues to accelerate. Leaders will need to be ever more adaptable and comfortable with uncertainty.

Focus on Well-being:

There's a growing recognition of the importance of mental health and well-being in the workplace. Leaders will need to prioritize employee wellness as a key component of organizational success.

Ethical Leadership:

In an era of increased transparency and social consciousness, there's a growing demand for ethical, authentic leadership.

Lifelong Learning:

With the rapid pace of change, continuous learning and upskilling will become even more critical for leaders.

Collaborative Ecosystems:

Organizations are progressively functioning as integral parts of larger ecosystems. Leaders must become adept at nurturing collaboration not only within their own organizations but also across various organizational boundaries.

These evolving dynamics indicate that the future of leadership will necessitate a heightened focus on emotional intelligence, adaptability, ethical decision-making, and the capacity to maneuver through complex, swiftly changing environments. The collaborative, emotionally intelligent leadership style we've examined in this book is poised to become even more vital in the years ahead.

Call to Action: Developing the Leaders of Tomorrow

As we complete this book, it's clear that the future of leadership is both exciting and challenging. To develop the leaders of tomorrow, organizations and individuals need to take proactive steps:

Invest in Emotional Intelligence:

Make EI a core component of leadership development programs. Provide tools and training for leaders to assess and improve their emotional intelligence.

Foster a Learning Culture:

Create an environment that encourages continuous learning and growth. This might include implementing mentoring programs, providing learning stipends, or creating internal "universities."

Embrace Diversity and Inclusion:

Make D&I a strategic priority. Develop programs to attract, retain, and promote diverse talent, and train leaders in inclusive leadership practices.

Develop Digital Literacy:

Ensure leaders are comfortable with emerging technologies and understand their potential impact on the business landscape.

From Command To Collaboration: A Journey In Modern Leadership

Emphasize Ethical Leadership:

Incorporate ethics and social responsibility into leadership development programs. Create clear ethical guidelines and model ethical behavior from the top down.

Practice Adaptive Leadership:

Train leaders in adaptive leadership techniques that allow them to navigate uncertainty and lead change effectively.

Prioritize Well-being:

Develop leaders who understand the importance of employee well-being and can create healthy, sustainable work environments.

Encourage Global Thinking:

Provide opportunities for leaders to gain international experience and develop cross-cultural competencies.

Focus on Purpose:

Help leaders connect their work and their teams' work to a larger, meaningful purpose. Train them in techniques for inspiring and motivating through purpose.

Build Collaborative Skills:

Enhance leaders' skills to cultivate collaboration both within their teams and across organizational boundaries.

For individual leaders, the imperative is to engage in continuous self-reflection and personal growth. Actively pursue constructive feedback, embrace diverse ideas and viewpoints, and commit to lifelong learning and development.

For organizations, it is essential to foster environments that promote these leadership attributes. This requires re-evaluating conventional hierarchies, recognizing and rewarding collaborative and emotionally intelligent behaviors, and investing in thorough, ongoing leadership training.

As we navigate an unpredictable future filled with intricate challenges and swift transformations, the caliber of our leadership will be crucial. By adopting a more collaborative, emotionally aware, and adaptable style of leadership, we can shape organizations that are not only more prosperous but also more compassionate and rewarding places to work.

The transition from military command to collaborative civilian leadership that we've examined in this book reflects the broader evolution occurring in the leadership landscape. By drawing lessons from this transition and dedicating ourselves to continuous growth and adaptation, we can develop leaders capable of guiding our organizations and society toward a more promising future.

Thank you for joining me on this exploration of modern leadership. May your own leadership journey be one of continuous learning, growth, and positive impact.